Welfare to Warden

Autobiography of the First
Woman in Michigan to Head
a Prison for Male Felons

This book is dedicated to:

Perry Johnson, who decided to introduce women into the Michigan Department of Corrections in a thoughtful and planned way, and who supported their journey and monitored their progress to guide them to success,

and Bill Kime, the love of my life, without whom there would have been no book,

and John Cordell, who inspired me to get my act together and has been a joy in my life,

and Luella Burke, Tekla Miller, and Denise Quarles, without whose support I would not have survived Jackson to become a warden.

Welfare to Warden

Pamela K. Withrow

Autobiography of the First Woman in Michigan to Head a Prison for Male Felons

Author: Pamela K. Withrow
Editor: Tanya Muzumdar
Designer: Kelly Ludwig
Cover design: Sarah Meiers

Readers are encouraged to go to www. MissionPointPress.com to contact the author or to find information on how to buy this book in bulk at a discounted rate.

MISSION POINT PRESS

Published by Mission Point Press
2554 Chandler Rd.
Traverse City, MI 49696
(231) 421-9513
www.MissionPointPress.com

ISBN: Hardcover: 978-1-958363-28-7
Softcover: 978-1-958363-29-4

Library of Congress Control Number: 2022915383

Printed in the United States of Americ

Welfare to Warden

Autobiography of the First
Woman in Michigan to Head
a Prison for Male Felons

CONTENTS

FOREWORD

"When I grow up, I want to be a prison warden."

How many people have you heard state that as their career path? My guess is not many. Add to it that the professional is a female, and I'd wager that number drops even lower.

The material in this book not only delves deeply into the journey of becoming a warden, it tackles the very challenging and difficult path of being a woman in a traditionally male-dominated field. Within these pages, she discusses the concept of concrete correctional practices, as well as the journey of a woman learning how to maneuver herself in a foreign work environment, with the aim of providing teachable moments to educate us all on how to be successful at both.

As a university educator and former warden, I found this book important in conveying correctional concepts in an easily digestible manner. As a woman, I found it touching, humorous, painful, and exhilarating as I walked along with Pam through her life and career.

Patty Barnhart, former prison warden, and lecturer, Arizona State University

INTRODUCTION

"But you don't look like a warden." After years of hearing this when someone was told I was a prison warden, I decided it was time to write a book about how this woman came to the work of prison administration. Because I was the first woman in Michigan and one of the first in the country to head a prison for men, I also thought my experience had historical significance.

And so follows a chronological history of how I, an Indiana farm girl, became the first woman to head a prison for men in Michigan. It describes the obstacles I overcame and innovations I introduced during a twenty-five-year career. It also includes anecdotes about prisoners as well as lessons I learned along the way.

I feel that my sometimes unconventional approaches to directing prison life might inspire others to take the road less traveled. For those curious about life inside the walls and fences of penal facilities, I will share information about incarceration, prisoners, and the people who do the tough work of operating correctional facilities. Appendices offer details about Michigan's correctional system for adults, cognitive work with offenders, and activities and events in my life.

When preparing the manuscript, I consulted calendars and journals. Both personal and professional events are described because each impacts the other. There is emphasis on the value of networking and support systems as well as the importance of professional organization membership. The role of the National Institute of Corrections and its Academy is noted.

The first and final chapters deal with events leading up to and following my career. These are included both as background and as a context for understanding my decision to leave interesting and fulfilling work at age fifty-two.

1. IN THE BEGINNING

Mother's favorite story from my childhood was a prayer I recited at about age three. It went something like this: "God bless Mommy and Daddy and baby Chere and Grandma and Grandpa and Aunt Ethel and Mitzi (the dog) and the cats...and I can take care of myself." She believed that attitude shaped my life. I grew up the oldest of four farm girls in a small, agricultural community near Lafayette, Indiana. The proximity of my paternal grandparents and a widowed great-aunt was a gift. It was almost impossible to get my mother and those in the other two households angry with me at the same time; someone was always welcoming and praising me. Since there was not a boy child to take over the farm, I was expected to pitch in as needed and can recall chasing pigs and cows in the mud and snow, helping make hay on hot August days, and carrying food and drink to my dad as he worked the fields.

From childhood, I was informed I was going to college and thus needed good grades in school. Fortunately, I learned to love reading at an early age. This skill was so valued that we were usually excused from chores if we were reading. That was a huge encouragement to a lazy kid! I recall hiding out in a tulip tree with a book, the bees buzzing around the flowers in the canopy, as my mother and grandmother called for me. If I did not come down when called, there might be a willow switch waiting, but the red stripes on my legs were worth those few more minutes with beloved books.

From age ten, when eligible to join, summers were consumed by 4-H. Although a weeklong camp experience held promise, the lure was primarily Myrtle Zollinger, a widow who lived in Lafayette and was sophisticated by our rural standards. She also made it clear that girls could do anything they wanted in life—a contradiction to the mantra, common in the 1950s, that women could be nurses, teachers, or secretaries. She encouraged me to step beyond the usual clothing and baking projects to try electricity and a competition called "Demonstration." This was a wonderful opportunity to take a subject, research it, and then provide a standup narrative and hands-on demonstration to judges. There were two projects I recall vividly: one showcased Master-Mix Brownies and the other, apples. The first was challenging for the family budget because of the ingredients. I am sure Mrs. Zollinger broke the rules when she offered federal-surplus butter for the many batches of brownie mix created. Finding the varieties of apples needed during the summer for the apple demonstration was also challenging. I was ready to give up, but she helped me find other ways to show that product—photos instead of the real thing. She was the first person to introduce me to what is called today "thinking outside the box." Her standards were high, but she was supportive. I like to think those were traits I chose to bring to the work of a warden.

Jackson Elementary School was small—only fourteen in my 8th-grade class—but put a high premium on learning. Mrs. Cox taught first grade there forever. The principal's office overlooked the central space formed by exterior elementary classrooms, except fifth grade. As part of the transition to junior high, fifth graders had a separate classroom on the top floor. There was a study hall with a small library for the junior high students. Oh, how we looked forward to moving to our place in the study hall, where the big kids set the standards for dress and deportment. Unfortunately, when I arrived, I was almost immediately in trouble. We had had the thrilling—and dreaded—health class on reproduction. This was sex-segregated and girls were issued gender-appropriate manuals. Study hall had desks with tops that lifted and no locks. Of course, Bruce McCormick, my nemesis, had to grab my manual and run around the study hall, waving it like a flag. I was fast and ran after him. We made several laps of the room before the principal was roused by the commotion. Even though it was not my fault, I was sentenced to the same detention period as Bruce. Detention for someone who rode the bus meant you had to arrange transportation home, which also meant you had to explain why you needed transportation; that led to grounding at home as well. Double jeopardy did not apply at our house.

Of course, school was not all academics. I was a cheerleader throughout junior high for basketball only, since this was Indiana. There was fierce rivalry among the five schools that would combine to form the high school. Many tears were shed when we failed to make the playoffs. The only time I can recall cheating in school was when the star basketball player copied my work. Our very demanding English teacher required that his students memorize the parts of speech and the rules governing grammar, and then write these in class. There was no way our star could remain academically eligible if he failed English. He had to practice for games and did not have time (or, I suspect, the aptitude) for rote memorization. I think the teacher guessed at our collusion in the star's successful completion of the assignment, but basketball being all-important in the Hoosier state, there was no inquiry.

We also had the opportunity to take band, music, and art. I learned to play the clarinet in band. The love of music led to a visit to Purdue University for a public radio broadcast where youngsters were challenged to identify classical compositions after hearing a few significant phrases. I think that was the first time my picture was in the *Lafayette Journal and Courier*, and such a fuss was made over it that I longed for more publicity. My sister, Chere, was an accomplished artist, and I recall drawing what I thought were beautiful leafless trees. The art teacher made it clear that these were not up to standard; being used to getting praise for my work, I dropped any attempt at art.

High school was both wonderful and frightening. I was smart, so the academics were not a problem, but my family was not well off. Homemade clothes were the norm at Jackson, but they were looked down on at Southwestern, the consolidated high school. I longed to belong to the cool clique; my grades and a wicked sense of humor made me marginally acceptable. I also drove to school most days, had a steady boyfriend, played saxophone in the dance band, and was involved in yearbook—all in the plus column. On the other hand, I got outstanding grades, was in science club, took Latin, chemistry, physics, and advanced algebra—all negatives. Thus, I was relegated to the fringes of the cool kids' group.

My vision was poor, and glasses heavy, with thick lenses. I desperately wanted contact lenses, but family finances did not include that luxury. My parents offered to pay for half the cost if I could figure out how to pay for the other half. Dad suggested pollinating corn, which was the best-paid work available for a youngster. It was also hot and itchy. The task was to put bags over the developing corn ears. Later, when the corn had grown tassels and silk, one bagged the tassels from one row and shook their pollen into the bag. That pollen was then applied to the silk of the ears from a different row. This was all done when the corn was much taller than the workers, with humidity near 100 percent and the sun scorching. While my friends rode on de-tasseling machines well above the cornstalks and got to wear next to nothing, I had to wear long sleeves and pants to avoid being cut to ribbons by the sharp leaves of the corn. I am convinced that job was designed to motivate college aspirations. It did.

When my parents decided to leave the family farm and move to Michigan the summer before my senior year, I jumped at the chance. Of course, there were elements holding me in Indiana. I had taken the responsibility of paid leadership of the 4-H group when Mrs. Zollinger retired, and her replacement burned out on kids and camp. Since I was not yet eighteen, I needed an adult to be the official leader, so Marge Gamble, who had led the club the previous year, agreed to share the duties (and the dollars). Her main objection was supervision of the club's members during camp, where the amenities were markedly absent. As the fates would have it, I was selected for Girls' State, a great leadership training opportunity and a real honor, except that it was the same week as 4-H camp. I consider it a mark of Marge's commitment to youth that she reconsidered her objection to going to camp and let me have the week at Girls' State. The other anchor in Indiana was my boyfriend at Purdue University. We had become pinned, a pre-engagement ritual, and I really was reluctant to live hours away from him; however, the potential for adventures in Michigan outweighed my passion. I was not yet ready to settle down.

My parents found a lovely ranch home with a pasture for Chere's horses; we had a sale of farm equipment in Indiana and moved to Michigan just before school started. Senior year at Haslett High was interesting, perhaps in the sense of the Chinese curse. I continued to excel academically and was voted by my classmates as Most Likely to Succeed. The relationship with my Purdue boyfriend did not survive; distance did not make the heart grow fonder. Before a winter dance, I recall a meeting in the girls' restroom where we divvied up the unattached males in the senior class. I drew Clint Cordell, an athlete who was known more for his jokes and storytelling than academic success. Clint and I hit it off and became a couple. I wrote for the school newspaper and recall fighting for journalistic freedom with a satirical column about the school counselor; it never made publication. My parents had started a rental business and were struggling financially; however, they continued to encourage me to go to college. Michigan State University admitted me, and the family somehow found the funds to permit me to live on campus. I enthusiastically signed up for a full slate of honors courses and looked forward to the fall.

Unfortunately, MSU was very crowded in 1967, and I was the third person assigned to a two-person suite with a pair of sophomores who clearly did not want me as a roommate. They invited me to a party where the agenda was to get freshmen drunk and in the bedrooms. I recall waking up in an elevator with an embarrassed young man asking me if I was all right. I was not. In fact, I was drunk and had been raped. It never occurred to me to go to the health clinic. Instead, I went back to the dorm, slept, and woke up hungover with only a sketchy recollection of the night before. I remembered enough, though, that I calmly slit my wrist. When the bleeding could not be stopped with available bandages, my roommates called the resident assistant, who made me go to the clinic. This was in 1967 and there were no rape protocols. No one asked me what had prompted the suicide attempt or referred me to a mental health professional. In one night, I was transformed from a bright-eyed, promising student to a pathetic mess. And that was how I saw myself for several years.

I went home with my parents, returning only to pack my room and arrange to quit school. I resumed my relationship with Clint, became pregnant at New Year's, married just after Valentine's Day, and became a mother to a son in September. My parents were understandably upset with these events; there are still gouges on the garage floor from the force of my father's axe as he split wood the night I told him I was pregnant and would marry Clint. Only years later did my mother disclose that a scholarship had been offered by MSU due to National Merit Semifinalist test scores.

Four years of marriage, with frequent separations, ended in divorce. I got a job as a long-distance telephone operator and returned to school—this time Lansing Community College. Since I was without funds, I took advantage of a federal program. The Law Enforcement Assistance Administration evolved from nationwide, racially motivated riots in the late '60s. Education of police officers was determined to be the remedy for racial insensitivity on the part of big-city police forces and I was a beneficiary. While those employed in law enforcement were given free books and tuition, plus money for childcare and travel to classes, aspiring officers were advanced the cost of books and tuition with the stipulation that the funds need not be repaid if the student worked in law enforcement for four years after graduation. Thus, I developed a burning desire to be a state trooper. Unfortunately, I did not investigate the qualifications, one of which was uncorrected 20/20 vision. Since the big E on an eye chart was a blur without glasses, I clearly would not make the cut. There was a sole female criminal justice instructor, Jane White, and she was supportive and encouraging. The other LCC instructors, however, counseled me out of law enforcement. They flattered me, saying I was too bright and too idealistic to be a good officer and should go to law school. This was, of course, music to my parents' ears. They had been a huge support as my marriage ended and continued to help me raise my son while I worked and attended classes. When the time came to transfer to MSU, I decided I could no longer work full time and go to school full time. I swallowed my pride and applied for welfare.

As far as I knew, nobody in my family had ever accepted aid from the government. Not only were my books and tuition federally funded, but now my living expenses were going to be provided by the state. There was even a program to provide childcare for my son, John, while I attended class. Of course, I had no car and no money for luxuries, but the absence of an auto contributed to my employment in the prison system. The bus driver on the route that passed Spartan Village, student housing where John and I lived, took pity on me one day when the grocery sack I was bringing home burst and discharged canned goods all over the ground. As he was helping me retrieve the groceries, he asked me out, and soon we were dating seriously. I graduated from MSU and moved to Ann Arbor for law school. Although LEAA no longer funded books and tuition, I could borrow money for that; I counted on the welfare system to provide living expenses. Washtenaw County was way ahead of the times in their standards for assistance. I still remember the meeting with my caseworker.

"You have a BA," she said.

"I do," I replied, "but I'm a full-time law student."

"Your son is in school all day. You need to find a job," was her response.

Now my degree was in multidisciplinary social science pre-law, with cognates in sociology, psychology, and philosophy—not really something you want to put on a resume. I asked the University of Michigan contact if there were options for part-time law students and was told there were not, so I withdrew from my studies in good standing with the stipulation that I could re-enroll anytime in the next five years. I returned to Lansing and Ingham County's less-restrictive welfare rolls. In the meantime, the bus driver boyfriend had moved to the mall-to-mall route in Lansing, which meant he had many state workers as passengers. He asked a bus full of passengers whether anyone was hiring and described my degree as criminal justice—which bordered on true, since I had focused on that while getting a general associate's degree at LCC. The records supervisor in the Department of Corrections' Central Office thought Corrections might be looking to hire women and suggested I see the affirmative action officer in Personnel.

Resume in hand, I went to Personnel, and was sent to see the superintendent of the Camp Program. The superintendent clearly was not interested and sent me packing. However, Personnel staff knew I was receiving welfare and was eligible for a program that would pay my salary for the first six months. The camps were chronically underfunded, and a free pair of hands interested the superintendent, who took me on. I married the bus driver, took the civil service test on a Saturday, and started my twenty-five-year career in corrections the following Monday.

2. CAMP HEADQUARTERS

Grass Lake was the mailing address of the camp headquarters where, on June 13, 1976, at age twenty-seven, I began work for the Michigan Department of Corrections. No lake was visible from the ugly concrete block building. I entered through a pale-green porch overhang that did look like it belonged on a lake cottage. The inside of the building was painted the same pale green and there had been no effort to disguise the concrete blocks. Only the superintendent's office had paneling to soften the utilitarian feel; the atmosphere conveyed that this was a no-nonsense place focused on getting the job done. Since there was no actual vacancy (recall that I was a welfare mom with a six-month stipend to make me attractive to employers), my first office was shared with an inmate clerk. My desk was even smaller than the inmate's and overlooked the fenced bus lot. My officemate was charged with teaching me his job so that I could take it over. He was a pleasant guy who seemed vaguely amused at his assignment. Across the hall was the records office, where I was directed to read inmate files to get a sense of the type of prisoner housed in the Camp Program and the way files were organized. This type of orientation was not isolated to the camps. As I was promoted to other positions, there was rarely any formal instruction, except for new corrections officers' training. I was fortunate to complete that program during my second job with the department. Otherwise, staff were trained by coworkers, prisoners, or simply left to fend for themselves by reading policy and procedure manuals and the employee handbook.

The records supervisor and the personnel officer were the only women in nonclerical jobs at camp headquarters, and I soon found that these two positions were often held by women. Prison counselor, my job title, on the other hand, was not a job for a woman in a male facility. That "counselor" title did not mean that I counseled prisoners. Camp Waterloo was next door and totally off-limits to women. The only prisoners I saw were the guys who cleaned the offices, and my officemate, who was soon out of a job. My initial tasks were to order eyeglasses and orthopedic shoes for camp prisoners. Jackson Prison, officially the State Prison of Southern Michigan, was the source of these commodities; the ordering process was convoluted. Delivery took so long that the prisoners were often transferred or paroled by the time the orders were delivered. If the prisoner had paroled or gone to a corrections center, tough! The budget of the Bureau of Correctional Facilities was separate from that of Field Services. If the offender had paroled or gone to a center, the shoes would go back to the factory and the eyeglasses would be returned to Optometry. If the prisoner had moved to another prison, I would have to manifest the item to his new facility and arrange transportation, usually through the Jackson transportation hub.

My coworkers were a mixed group. The superintendent was a corrections professional who tried to run his small empire in a responsible way and hold staff accountable. The deputy seemed to be marking time until retirement; he ignored me. The treatment director also saw his work as a profession and took me under his wing, attempting to fill in the gaps of my education. Since I had never had a class dealing with corrections, that was a yawning chasm. The classification director was the only person actively rude to me. He made it clear that he did not think women should be working with male prisoners and that our presence was disruptive to the good order needed to operate an effective facility. This seemed a little over the top, considering that the camps were really a collection of small prisons, and I was working at headquarters, not dealing with offenders. However, his attitude prepared me for a mindset I would encounter repeatedly.

The program coordinator was another warm body waiting to retire. He was pleasant but dismissive. His job was to screen prisoners for the three programs of most interest to them: Corrections Center, Work Pass, and Furloughs. Corrections centers were in urban areas. Nonviolent offenders could be placed in these settings for as long as three years prior to parole. A center was looked at as a stepping-stone to parole and a coveted status. Work Pass operated from selected camps and was an opportunity for offenders to work in the private sector, typically for minimum wage. Although the work was usually hard and dirty or dull and repetitive, it was much better than the assignments available within the prison, which typically paid less than a dollar a day. Furloughs were another test for parole and ranked nearly as high as a center placement in the inmate culture. A furlough was a forty-eight-hour pass home with a responsible relative. Prisoners were prohibited from drinking alcohol or using drugs, and had to remain with a responsible person at the designated home location, except when traveling to and from camp. When I was initially involved with furloughs, there were no tests for drugs or alcohol except the camp staff doing a whiff test of the prisoner's breath when he returned. I suspect there was some heavy partying that went undetected.

Soon after starting work at the Camp Program, I found that the superintendent and special programs director were carpooling from Lansing daily. Since I did not have reliable transportation, I was happy to contribute a few dollars for gas and be driven to work in a comfortable van. An auxiliary benefit was that my corrections education continued for the two hours of travel daily, as the superintendent shared his experiences on the parole board and at facilities. His stories were sometimes cautionary tales—your reputation will be damaged forever if you offer rioting inmates steak and ice cream—and other times just funny or sad recollections of staff or prisoners he had come to know over the years. What was most useful was that he did not demonize offenders. He made it clear that they were people, often damaged by their life experiences. The ones we were responsible for were headed for the street; therefore, we had better do what we could to sort out those who could be safely returned from those who needed more time to reflect on their mistakes and learn how to be good citizens. He was clear that education and work were the experiences that would convert offenders from criminals to responsible members of society.

A few months passed, and I discovered a regular cribbage game at lunchtime in the superintendent's office. Occasionally, a regular player would be absent, and I would sit in. I was good at the game, and the superintendent was interested in winning. Soon I found myself partnered with him and becoming part of the work culture. Then the program coordinator retired. I interviewed for, and got, that position. I was officially part of the camps, no longer in a make-work job. I got to keep the orthopedic shoes and eyeglasses tasks and added the program coordinator's duties. This opened a new window in the corrections business. Although the camp superintendent was authorized to approve furloughs, applications for Corrections Center had to be further screened and approved by Tony Balice in Lansing's corrections headquarters. Work Pass applications had to be reviewed and approved by JoAnn Bach. Now I had two contacts in Lansing who knew me and my work.

The most fun I had in the camp program was at the quarterly staff meetings. These were held at the McMullen Training Center near Higgins Lake State Park and brought all the camp supervisors together for two days of meetings during the day and hard partying at night. Here my corrections education continued, since most of the supervisors had worked at one of Michigan's old penitentiaries (Jackson, Marquette, or the Reformatory) prior to their promotion to head a camp. They related that prisoners are generally easy to manage, especially in minimum security; the challenge is to manage staff. That truth was reinforced again and again as I moved into supervisory roles.

The record office supervisor, Sally, and I became friends. She was a good golfer and complained to me that the annual golf outing for corrections was not open to women. I looked at the flyer announcing the event and could not find anything that specified gender, so told her I would go and drive the cart if she signed up to golf. We both went, had fun, and broke that gender barrier.

After less than a year in the camps, I received a call asking me to go to Lansing and interview with the deputy director in the Program Bureau. I knew about that bureau, as I had made it my business to understand the organization chart and the functions of all the bureaus and offices. Nonetheless, I was puzzled about the call and wondered why they wanted to talk to me. It was a day away from work and a chance to visit Central Office, so I went.

»»»»»»»»»»»

Lesson Learned: I had an unpleasant conversation with an employee at another prison whom I felt had wronged me. I fired off an angry letter without consulting my supervisor. The recipient sent it, along with a response, to the superintendent who simply asked me whether, in hindsight, sending the letter was a good idea. On reading my original missive, I was embarrassed. It was juvenile and petty. I told him I was wrong to send it. He agreed. I wrote to the person I had offended and apologized. I learned to sit on anything written in the heat of emotion.

»»»»»»»»»»»

Corrections Story: The prisoners who worked at Camp Control were pleasant and polite. I was curious about their living conditions. Their camp supervisor often visited Camp Control and I asked him many questions about his operation. He was a bit of a renegade and, one day, offered to show me around the camp. I knew the unwritten rule that women did not go there but could not resist the chance. Off we went, right through the forbidden door and into his domain. Long dormitories, lined with bunks, comprised the living quarters. There was a dining hall, kitchen, offices, and a visiting area. I do not recall much more about that visit, except that I detected the faint odor of marijuana. When I commented about that, he did not even pause—said it was not a big problem and kept the inmates quiet.

3. THE PROGRAM BUREAU

After nearly nine months at camp headquarters, I was called to the Stevens T. Mason Building in Lansing, which housed Corrections's Central Office, for an interview with Bill Kime, the deputy director of the Program Bureau, and his assistant. We met in the director's conference room, an impressive, paneled room with shelves of statutes, law books, and manuals, barely leaving room for the comfortable high-backed chairs surrounding the largest conference table I had ever seen. During introductions, it became clear that I was there to interview for a research vacancy. For what seemed like an eternity, I waited for that interview to begin. Deputy Director Kime extolled the virtues of the position: it offered various duties, so it was interesting; it permitted travel at state expense; it involved visiting many institutions, thus offering opportunities to meet staff throughout the Department of Corrections (DOC) and, most importantly, it gave access to the leaders of the DOC. The assistant did not add much to this sales pitch. One of them, though, finally asked, "Are you interested?" Of course I was interested! I could take a bus to work and end the hour-long commute, and it was a great opportunity. When I answered yes, they congratulated me and said a start date would be arranged. It was the strangest non-interview I had ever experienced.

When I reported for the first day of work, Deputy Director Kime said things were a little slow and that I should read files for a while to get a feel for the kinds of work the Program Bureau handled and the way reports were presented. He offered two three-shelf lateral files, each about four feet long, and suggested I begin with anything that looked interesting. Well, everything looked interesting, so I started at the beginning and worked my way through all the files. It took about a month. When I was done, I reported that to Kime; his response was, "All of them?" Well, he then found a small project for me that involved some basic research and a simple report. I finished that and submitted it through my nominal boss, Kime's assistant. It was returned with only a few red-pen suggestions from Kime. The assistant expressed his dismay that so little was found wanting; I later discovered that he was not a strong writer and that his submissions usually were returned with lots of arrows, deletions, and rewording. That this new kid on the block had managed to generally satisfy his boss had to have been galling. Of course, since I had just spent a month reading files, I had a good idea of the kind of writing the bureau produced and had tried to keep my report consistent with that standard. Kime was happy; his assistant was not. That was to be true the whole of my tenure in Lansing.

Several happy connections were made during my time in the Program Bureau. Susan Hunter was introduced to me while she was doing work toward her PhD at Michigan State University. She was not yet working in corrections; however, she was an early advocate for networking and increasing diversity in the profession. Susan encouraged me to join the American Correctional Association and attend their conferences. We took an instant liking to each other and I looked forward to crossing paths with her in the future. Replacing me at the camp headquarters was Luella Burke. We got to know each other through phone conversations and conferences of the Michigan Corrections Association. Another piece of good fortune was meeting Bob Berles, the department's treatment director. He introduced me to Lawrence Kohlberg's theory of stages of moral development. I was grateful to have found out about that so early in my career. It framed my initial dealings with offenders and helped me understand why they seemed so immature in their thinking.

Other assignments came quickly. The director needed an update to an assessment of new officer training. Since female corrections officers were still relatively new to the DOC, he suggested to Kime that I might be the right person for that task. Off I went to new officer training, which was conducted in Jackson at one of the many homes no longer used to house high-ranking prison officials. In 1977, corrections officers received two weeks of training in the classroom and then were sent to the prison where they would be assigned for on-the-job training, which included firearms qualifications. The training director had been told about my assignment, but none of the trainers knew I was evaluating their performance. Naturally, the rest of the new officer trainees, all male by the way, were also kept in the dark. Because corrections ran a lean operation in those days, I did not plan to spend all the on-the-job training days at the State Prison of Southern Michigan, Central Complex, my assigned prison. There was work waiting for me at the Program Bureau and I was writing the assessment as the training progressed. So, I went to my assigned position for a few days and then went to Lansing for a day. When I returned to the prison, the captain directed me to report to him after roll call. Roll call consisted of lines of officers standing at attention in the central rotunda while the command staff shouted assignments and information relevant to the day's work. New officers were generally assigned to areas staffed by more experienced officers and shown the ropes by those officers. The old hands at the prison assured me this was an improvement on their introduction to the work. In earlier times, not only was there no classroom training for officers, on-the-job training was often performed by the inmate clerk after the officer being relieved handed over his keys.

What the captain wanted to see me about was the previous day's absence. I had assumed that he knew of my assignment as a training evaluator. It turned out that he did not know, or care, about that. He proceeded to dress me down thoroughly. When he ran out of steam, it was clear to me that the proper way to miss a day as an officer was to call the control center at the prison and explain the reason for being absent. This experience prepared me for many instances in the future when incomplete or inconsistent communications would cause problems. Whether written or verbal, clear, complete communication is essential to getting prison work done right. It became my mission to make sure staff with whom I worked got information from me that would make it easier, not harder, to get the job done.

My stint at Jackson opened my eyes to officer involvement in prisoner misconduct. One of the approved assignments for a female officer was the visiting room. While assigned there, I observed a prisoner exchange shoes with a visitor. When I brought it to the attention of the experienced officer working with me, she responded that new shoes are hard to get in prison and that was one of the ways prisoners got good footwear. Since I knew nothing about how prisoners got personal clothing, I accepted her response; however, I later asked one of the supervisors about the event and he assured me that it was a violation and told me that the prisoner was probably getting drugs as well as new shoes in that transaction. On another occasion, the same female officer permitted a prisoner and his female visitor to occupy the bathroom at the same time, although they did not enter together. Even though I was a "fish" (new officer or new prisoner), I knew this was not right and advised her that a mistake had occurred. We had a prisoner and his visitor in the bathroom together. She had to intervene, and I allowed her to save face by calling it a mistake. I had learned another prison survival skill: calling a violation a mistake when dealing with a peer permits you to identify a problem and let the other person fix it before you both get into trouble. The last time I was in the company of that same female officer was while heading for the officers' dining room. As she passed a prisoner in the hall, I heard her call out that she would pick up that carton of squares at the end of the shift. I may have been a fish, but I knew she was referring to a carton of cigarettes. I also knew that prisoners treated these as currency and that she was being paid off for permitting a rule violation. I reported all these events to the shift supervisors but have no way of knowing whether any disciplinary action ensued. In later years, when discussing my observations with her coworkers and supervisors, I found that she was generally known to be colluding with prisoners to break the rules, and was so good at it that she was never caught. I also know that this officer later earned a degree and became a supervisor, which is a sad testament to the practice of rewarding education and longevity with promotion, without regard to character issues.

In addition to the new officer school evaluation, I was involved in activities related to the expansion of the prison system. Due to a wave of baby-boom offenders entering the crime-prone years, which resulted in a significant rise in the crime rate, the DOC was receiving more prisoners than available housing could accommodate. Deputy Director Kime had described this in an analogy: he suggested that I think of a bus. There are a finite number of seats on that bus; if the number getting on matches the number getting off, there are always enough seats. When the number getting on (in our case, prison commitments) or the number getting off (parolees) do not match, you end up with too few or too many seats. In the late 1960s and early 1970s, the prison population had been so low that the Reformatory was able to close entire floors. That was not the case in the late 1970s. Crowding caused the DOC to look at a variety of quick-fix housing solutions. Mental health was moving in the direction of community treatment, so closed mental health facilities were considered for conversion to prisons. Riverside, in Ionia, had space suitable for a reception center for younger prisoners. Since the two prisons designated for youthful prisoners were in Ionia (the Michigan Reformatory and the Michigan Training Unit), the Program Bureau was asked to develop a program statement for this proposed reception center.

It was a great assignment which involved a review of the intake processes at the existing Reception Center at Jackson and then the design of an intake process at Riverside. Space constraints at Riverside demanded a quicker turnaround than was the norm at Jackson. As I asked questions about the lengthy process at Jackson, I uncovered bottlenecks that had frustrated staff. When these were resolved, both reception facilities could function more efficiently. This experience helped me understand the need for process review generally, since it is only through questions that issues are identified. Absent questions, the inertia of the system will be sustained, and the operation will have a mantra: "This is the way we've always done it."

Another fun, although mundane, assignment involved the conversion of Kincheloe Air Force Base in Sault Ste. Marie to Kinross Correctional Facility. As part of the transition, the DOC had agreed to inventory equipment in the spaces we were acquiring. So, I got to fly up to the Soo on a state plane and count chairs and other items while my colleague, the agency's conversion expert, determined how best to use the buildings we were getting. Before we had partnered with the military, inmate housing was generally of two types: single cells (with in-cell sinks and toilets) in high security, or large dormitories. The dorms were ideally used for housing low-security prisoners, although crowding had forced some of the facilities to convert dayrooms or bulkheads (dead space in cellblocks) to congregate housing. At Kinross, the rooms were too large for one or even two prisoners, so three-man rooms became the third type. As we continued to convert existing facilities to meet the need for space, a variety of nontraditional configurations would emerge. Prisoners usually preferred their own cell or room, but most would accept dorms and shared rooms for the increased freedom offered by lower security.

An offshoot of the expansion process was the public hearing. Deputy Director Kime usually handled these, along with others in high positions; however, when the DOC was exploring converting a small military installation to a minimum-security camp, Kime thought it would be a good strategy to send me to conduct the hearing. I had worked in the camp system and, as a woman, might be accorded more civility than the agency had been experiencing in other communities. In Saugatuck, for example, where a Catholic seminary was being considered for conversion, the director was hanged in effigy and the state police were on hand to quell a potential disturbance at a heated public hearing where most community members opposed the establishment of that prison. It is a truth that citizens want lawbreakers behind bars— they just do not want a prison in their community. Kime's strategy was not successful. Citizens did not want a camp in their community, and they were very vocal about it. I had my first experience of public anger directed at me as a representative of the DOC; it was not enjoyable. However, it was part of the process of learning to absorb others' anger and understanding that it was not personal. I was simply the available representative and thus got the abuse.

»»»»»»»»»»»»

While socializing outside work when I was at the camp headquarters was limited to a Christmas party, Central Office was party central. Most Friday nights featured after-work drinking, often at the home of one or another of the deputy directors. I learned that these were called POETS parties, not because they involved poetry, but because the acronym meant "P— on Everything,

Tomorrow's Saturday." While most learning took place during office hours, I also gained knowledge at the after-work gatherings. With alcohol as a lubricant, people would tell stories about the work of corrections—and sometimes the misdeeds of coworkers. It was at one of these parties that I heard about the warden who had smashed up his state car while driving under the influence. The car was taken to a prison with an auto-body repair vocational program, fixed and painted, and returned to the warden without any formal report to Central Office. I discovered that another warden, who was promoted to a desk in the hall in Central Office until he decided to retire, had received that "promotion" because of his ill-treatment of his assistant deputy, who leapfrogged over him to become the deputy director in charge of all the prisons. The lesson there was to be fair to everyone because you never knew who your boss would be. The other thing I learned at those parties, and in my day-to-day dealings, was that the people in Central Office are regular folks who struggle with problems and issues. They have experience and knowledge that suit them for their jobs, but they are not miracle workers and do not have all the answers. The last thing I learned was that I was not suited for Central Office. Long meetings that left issues unresolved were frustrating to me; I have one of those faces unsuitable for poker—what I am thinking is written all over it. When what you are thinking is something like, "Will this meeting never end?" or "Why can't someone just make a decision so we can move on?" you know you need to find a different job.

Fortunately, whenever I was asked what I would like to do next, I had always responded, "Work as a camp supervisor." That answer was probably a product of my familiarity with the camps and affection for those who worked at Camp Control; however, it seemed to me that running one of those mini-prisons was just one of the coolest jobs in existence and that it would be fun and interesting to do it. What I was not considering was that all twelve camps housed male prisoners and all those prisoners were supervised by male staff. One product of being the oldest girl on a family farm with no boys is that you do whatever needs to be done. I had been a feminist without knowing what one was, but happily acknowledged that label during my college years. It just did not occur to me that a woman could not be a camp supervisor. When Director Perry Johnson decided that I would become the supervisor at Camp Brighton, I was unprepared for the controversy and publicity that accompanied that appointment.

Lesson Learned: Know what job you want next, tell anyone who asks that you want that job, and prepare yourself for that position.

Corrections Story: Part of the new officer school that I was dreading was touring the cell blocks inside Jackson. As the only woman in the class, I feared I would be subjected to catcalls and other abuse. As it turned out, there was a slender young man in the class who wore his blond hair in a style well below his collar. The inmates singled him out, with calls of "Blondie, blondie, blondie," and offers that were quite obscene in nature. The young man returned to class the next day with a buzz cut.

4. CAMP BRIGHTON

To my amazement, I had been named supervisor of Camp Brighton after only a year in the Program Bureau. While I had consistently stated a desire to be a camp supervisor whenever anyone asked, I did not expect I would get my dream job any time soon. I had observed the department's promotional practices, and it seemed to me that you had to be around quite a while before being promoted. However, not one to turn down an opportunity to advance, I accepted the promotion and returned to camp headquarters for direction. I had never been to Camp Brighton and hoped the deputy, who was my boss, would escort me there and introduce me to the staff. He did not offer to do so. Thus, I headed off alone. I was met by a reporter/photographer from the Brighton Argus who interviewed and snapped photos of me at the camp with a very pregnant beagle, who appeared to be the camp mascot. I had had no formal training in dealing with the media and just tried to answer questions honestly and without much elaboration. Of course, the fact that I was not escorted by the deputy and had been met by the media before I had even had a chance to meet the staff did not get things off to a good start.

When I entered the main office, I asked staff to describe the function of the count board, thus displaying my ignorance about the most basic activity of the camp—taking count. The lieutenant, a genial older man whom I later learned had agreed to train me in camp operations, suggested we move into the interior office. He introduced himself and described the other supervisory staff. There was a sergeant, whom I would meet at 4:00 p.m. He supervised the afternoon shift; the final supervisor was a corporal, who directed the midnight shift. The lieutenant was responsible for the 8:00 – 4:00 shift; my job was to direct the activities of the three shift supervisors, manage camp operations, and provide counseling to the prisoners.

Brighton housed 140 adult male minimum-security prisoners who worked or attended school. No inmates were permitted to stay in the camp if they were unfit for an assignment. Not only did the camp provide workers for the Department of Natural Resources parks in the area, but it also had a large crew working DNR's nursery operation. There were prisoners who went into the community on Work Pass—a form of work release from the camp. Work Pass jobs were highly sought, as these prisoners made minimum wage, which permitted them to save for release. In contrast, offenders working for the DNR or in camp assignments made less than $1 daily, which barely kept them in commissary supplies.

Most people think of prisons being about the offenders and, while it is true that the purpose of prisons is to protect the public by keeping prisoners incarcerated and offering them opportunities to change through education and other programs, prison managers generally agree that it is the staff who make operating prisons a challenge. My small staff of eleven was no exception to that truth. When the sergeant arrived, he, the lieutenant, and I went into the inner office, which I later learned was called the "pine box." Standing at six feet, two inches to my five feet, four inches, the sergeant commenced his comments using theatrical gestures. He assured me that he would give me his usual 110 percent until I hanged myself, and then he wanted to be the one to pull the trap door. There were three of us standing in the small office. Feeling somewhat intimidated, I said that I hoped he would give me a chance and then turned to the lieutenant for more transitional information. He did not fail me and continued his description of camp operations as if nothing had happened.

What no one had told me, and which I should have known enough to ask, were the circumstances which created the opening at Camp Brighton. Who was my predecessor, why did he leave, and where was he now? I say "he" because I was the first woman to head a male camp—thus the Argus interview. Well, it turned out that the previous supervisor, who was Black, had lost the confidence of his staff by siding with prisoners in matters of camp operations, even after being cautioned by the staff that his decisions were undermining the security of the facility. While minimum-security prisoners were primarily white, there were enough Black offenders (and no other Black staff) that there were questions of whether race was a factor in the staff's dissatisfaction. The sergeant had taken it upon himself to go to the deputy director to complain about the supervisor's actions, skipping two rungs of the chain of command in the paramilitary organization. When that did not fix the problem, the sergeant and other staff had participated in a sick-out. The supervisor and lieutenant were the only ones willing to come to the facility. Well, two people cannot operate a three-shift camp for long, so the supervisor was sent to a different prison to be a special projects coordinator and I replaced him. Staff later told me that the appointment of a white woman was even more objectionable than that of a Black man, so they understood the message—work with her or else! Of course, that did not stop the obstreperous sergeant from saying his piece.

As time passed, I settled into the rhythm of the camp. During the day, the lieutenant and one officer handled getting the prisoners into the "green dogs" (military green, canvas-covered stake-rack trucks the DNR used to transport their workers) and supervising those who stayed at the camp. A few prisoners who had not completed their GED (high-school equivalency) also attended school. Staff provided security only. Prisoner workers cooked, provided routine maintenance, cleaned, staffed the medical dispensary and gym, and handled grounds care. There were no fences, although a previous supervisor had planted quite a bit of multiflora rose (a particularly tenacious, rambling, thorny bush) which gave us clues as to who had been offsite to pick up drugs or alcohol, since the miscreant often returned with scratched hands and ankles.

Off-grounds workers returned after the 4:00—12:00 shift had arrived and were always pat-searched to detect contraband. Occasionally, especially if the scent of marijuana had been detected, all incoming prisoners would be strip-searched in the visiting room. As a female, I did not participate in these searches—my job was to staff the office and see whether anything was thrown out the windows of the visiting room. And, of course, prisoners did try to get rid of contraband before staff found it on them. We really did not care whether we identified the culprit trying to bring in drugs or other contraband, we simply wanted to keep it out of the camp. The state police served as our arresting agency, and we had to observe chain-of-evidence rules to be able to testify in court if the offender did not plead out. As you might guess, court with our bare-bones staffing resulted in overtime, which we tried to avoid. Since all prisoners were "home" in the evening, the afternoon shift had three or four staff.

Lights were out at midnight on the weekends and 11:00 p.m. during the week. The two or three staff present for the night shift had only to ensure things stayed quiet and no one escaped. This was accomplished by counts, roughly an hour apart, throughout the night at irregular times. One night the count came up long. Staff feared being short, because that meant turning on all the lights, counting everyone on their bunk, and, often, searching for an escapee. However, no one could recall being over count. It turned out that one of the offenders had smuggled his girlfriend into the dorm and stashed her in a vacant bunk when staff made an unannounced count. That was the talk of the camp for quite some time! Escapes were not common; nevertheless, one unusual factor was that when a prisoner did escape, it was frequently when he was close to going to the corrections center or home on parole. When I asked more experienced staff about this, they acknowledged the pattern, but they had no explanation. I have also puzzled about this, but can find no rationale for conduct which, when the offender was captured and prosecuted, would lead to five more years in a secure prison. And almost all were returned to prison.

Another thing that I noticed after a while was that familiar faces reappeared. One man was at the camp three different times during my three-and-a-half years at Brighton. Staff called this "doing life on the installment plan." I thought I had begun to know the offender well enough by his third visit to ask him what was happening that led to his reincarceration. He suggested it was the fault of the system—he could handle supervision in the camp, but just did not like the reporting requirements on parole and failed to show up for appointments with his agent. Since the agent could still find him on his job or at his home, he would quit his job, move out of his authorized living arrangement, and then be involved in more crime to support himself. While this did not seem to me to justify his belief that it was the system's fault he was returning to prison, he clearly believed that was the truth. When this prisoner left the last time, the camp counselor and I called him into the pine box and told him we had a bet on how long he would last on the street this time. Perhaps that challenge was what did it or maybe he was tired of doing time, but that prisoner is one of a few who stayed in touch with me over the years. Every three or four years, I would hear from him and he would bring me up to date on his activities (which seemed to me to be marginally criminal) and taunt me that both the counselor and I had lost our bet because he had not returned to prison. Maybe we had discovered a key to reducing recidivism; however, I think it was effective only in this case.

Well, the staff decided to give me a chance. I told them I knew people in Lansing and at Camp Control who could help us make camp life better and that I would work those angles if they would teach me to run a camp, so we came to an accommodation. Things were going well for several months and then—disaster! The lieutenant, who was the only actively supportive staff member, separated a shoulder trying to break a horse and was unable to return to prison work. I was left with the sergeant as acting lieutenant. As quickly as possible, I hired a permanent replacement. While the sergeant had potential, there was no way I could make him lieutenant so soon after his confrontational greeting. Instead, I hired an experienced lieutenant who kept the camp running well while I learned the craft of camp supervisor, which included being the counselor to 140 prisoners. The dual responsibilities of staff supervision and counseling offenders were challenging. I was glad I had been told to read inmate files and had gained experience with Furlough, Work Pass, and Correction Center applications during my first assignment in Camp Control. At least I knew the rudiments of those processes. I learned to write parole eligibility reports and how to prepare offenders to meet with the parole board.

During a parole board hearing, a prisoner who had been involved in a brutal crime in which a homeowner and his wife had been killed, accepted responsibility for his role in the death of the husband but insisted that the wife was an old lady who just died. The parole board gave him a year-long continuance on that and a subsequent visit. Prior to the third hearing, I convinced the prisoner that the fact that he had hit the woman over the head with a fireplace poker, resulting in her long-term hospitalization, which led to blood clots that caused the stroke that killed her, did mean he had some responsibility for her death. At his third interview, he rather grudgingly told the parole board member that he was sorry the old woman died, and parole was granted.

This same prisoner served as the camp nurse, passing over-the-counter medications to prisoners with minor complaints and bandaging minor injuries. Due to the emphasis on work assignments, all offenders needed to be able to work; those who were too often unable to perform were reassigned, usually to a northern camp. Consequently, most maintained good health. We noticed, however, that there was a serious uptick in the numbers of offenders reporting to the infirmary for medications. This change corresponded with the theft of instant coffee from the commissary. The sergeant drove himself crazy shaking down both locations trying to find out how the carefully controlled coffee was being stolen and how the inmate nurse was hiding it. Finally, we found that the nurse was hiding the coffee in plain sight—it was inside one of the huge brown bottles used to store bulk medication. Since it rattled around like the medication it was supposed to be, and the sergeant had not opened every container in the infirmary during the searches, it probably would not have been found without the cooperation of a prisoner who was leaving the camp. The theft of the instant coffee was through the metal back of the locked cabinet in which it was stored.

We had several conversations with Prison Industries about the security issues presented by their flimsy cabinets. A padlock on the front is not effective if the prisoners can easily peel off the cabinet back. Both the nurse and the head cook had to be fired, which was a sad day for the camp. The cook was a genius in making the food sent from Camp Control into palatable meals, and the nurse was trusted by prisoners to diagnose and treat their minor ailments. As I recall, we just switched their job assignments because they were the most competent prisoners we had, and it was understood that offenders test staff's best efforts to maintain security.

Two other prisoners were especially memorable. The first was a slight young man coming from Jackson. He had a shaved head and a large rose tattooed above one ear. I called him into my office for an interview and queried him about his unusual presentation. "Oh," he said, "now that I'm in camp, I'll let my hair grow out and the tattoo won't show. I acted crazy at Jackson to stay safe. I won't have to do that here." I smile every time I think of his creative solution to ensure his survival at Jackson. The second prisoner was an attractive, well-spoken young man from Oakland County who spent his spare time playing tennis. He had robbed a local Clark gas station, where he was known to the staff, and ridden away on his bicycle. Naturally, he was located, charged, and promptly convicted. His family visited regularly and, since this was his first offense, he was paroled at the first opportunity. Back on the streets, he returned to the same Clark station, robbed it, and rode away on his bicycle. He hanged himself in the jail while awaiting trial. I thought I had known this prisoner, but he clearly had some demons he was able to keep under wraps. Prisoners who had also known him during his stay at Brighton were similarly mystified at his suicide, so I was not the only one fooled by his sunny demeanor.

When, for the second time, I hired a lieutenant from outside the camp instead of promoting the sergeant, he got the message that he would get the lieutenant's job only when he became an ally instead of an antagonist. While I still was not as good a supervisor as I would become, I had won over some staff by working double shifts during deer season, so the officers who hunted could take time off and go "up north." As promised, my contacts in Central Office and Camp Control were helpful in greasing the wheels when we needed things. As an example, I had come to know the department's conversion specialist while working in the Program Bureau. He determined how to make what had been an Air Force base, a mental hospital, or a seminary into a prison. He also had to help figure out how to get furnishings for the new prisons when we were in tight budget times. One of his sources was state surplus, a dumping ground for used furniture and equipment from state agencies. Well, what some in civil service thought was junk was a prize for Camp Brighton. We made several trips, based on his tips, to upgrade office and visiting-room furnishings. I was also able to expedite Work Pass and Center applications, based on contacts in Camp Control and Central Office.

Best of all, the friends I had made in Central Commissary were willing to distribute emergency toilet paper when we ran low on that critical commodity. Believe it or not, the absence of toilet paper is a crisis in a prison. This versatile item can be used not only for the intended purpose, but as facial tissue, napkins, picture-hanging goop (mixed with a little glue), shoe sizing (the camps were notorious for ill-fitting shoes), baggies for medication (and sometimes illicit drugs), and even papier mâché. This last use I discovered the first Christmas at the facility, when little snowmen started to appear as decorations. Perhaps this was a clue about the sudden shortage of toilet paper!

At Camp Brighton, I was made aware of the intense sadness of the holiday season in prison. While people in the free world are preparing to celebrate with friends and family, prisoners must steel themselves for the reality that they may not get a visit on Christmas, even from their moms. In many cases, the male parent has been long gone from the offender's life. To counter the somber mood, we offered really good food for a prison and permitted special items to be brought in on visits during the month of December. Additional deposits in the prisoners' accounts were also permitted, and the prisoner store stocked seasonal and luxury gifts so the prisoners could treat themselves with their extra funds. Even these efforts did little to soften the reality of separation from loved ones, and staff had to be especially vigilant for suicide attempts during the holidays.

As I have mentioned, staff pose the biggest challenge to prison administrators and my group was no exception. Even though the camp was a minimum-security facility, and most offenders were going home within a year, staff were still very security conscious and would raise security issues with every change proposed. I was talking one afternoon with a pastor who offered Protestant services to interested prisoners. Both he and I had noticed the "poor me" attitude most Brighton residents portrayed. Even though they were the perpetrators of robberies, burglaries, auto thefts, drunk driving, and occasionally homicides, almost all characterized their activities as something they had to do and saw their apprehension and incarceration as a wrong imposed upon them by society. The attitude of the robber who had killed the husband and wife was typical—he and his partner just wanted the goods rumored to be in the home. If the husband had not tried to interfere, they would not have had to kill him, and if the wife had not tried to save her husband, they would not have had to hurt her, leading to her death. It was the victims' fault that they had died and put the poor prisoner away for all these years. If they had just given them what they wanted, the robbers would have gone away without anyone being harmed. After all, insurance covers stolen stuff, so that does not count as harm. The pastor and I brainstormed ways we might help prisoners get past this kind of thinking, and he suggested that they could benefit from volunteering at Hillcrest. This was a mental health facility where his parishioners often volunteered. It was only about fifteen minutes from the camp and chronically short-staffed. He thought Hillcrest would welcome extra pairs of hands, even prisoners', to work with the severely handicapped and developmentally disabled young people housed there.

Well, staff did not think this was a good idea at all and raised several objections. First, and probably most importantly, there were lots of female staff who might be accosted by the prisoner volunteers. Second, someone would have to transport prisoners, and we could not spare the staff. Finally, nobody had ever done anything like this before, so it was probably just a bad idea and presented an unnecessary security risk by putting prisoners on the road after dark. These discussions helped me develop the arguments I would need to sell the idea to my supervisor at Camp Control. I told him we wanted to conduct a pilot project for ninety days to see if improved prisoner behavior was a result. I would work from noon until 8:30 p.m. and transport the prisoners, leaving all assigned staff at the facility. The project would involve fifteen prisoners, going out in groups of five each week. To be eligible, prisoners had to be misconduct-free for several months and continue good conduct or be dismissed from the program. He could not find a good objection. Interestingly enough, no one asked about the success or failure of the program, which continued well beyond the pilot's ninety days.

We helped Hillcrest residents bounce on trampolines, go sledding, play in the snow, create craft items, and make and eat ice-cream sundaes. It was interesting to me to see a macho male prisoner tenderly wipe the face of an ice-cream-covered resident or bounce with and smile encouragingly at a resident on the trampoline. The best times for me were the return to the camp. In the dark of the van, the offenders would talk about the lack of options for Hillcrest residents and how many opportunities prisoners had for a fresh start when released. There were many variations on this theme, but, as the pastor and I had hoped, their time as volunteers had helped this group of prisoners move from their victim attitude to one of possibilities.

On no occasion did I hear a complaint about any prisoner's behavior. In fact, when the time for the Special Olympics competition in Howell came, Hillcrest supervisors asked whether I might bring all fifteen program participants so that they would have enough support for the number of residents they wanted to take. This idea was both wonderful and terrifying. I could not supervise all fifteen prisoners myself. I had to ask staff to volunteer to change days off and schedules so we would have enough coverage to run the camp as well as transport and supervise the prisoners at Howell High School. To my delight, that part went smoothly. Another scary element was the unpredictability of offender behavior. While we had had no problems so far, this event was to be held on a glorious spring day at a high school where many scantily dressed young women would be present, and, to add a little spice, Howell was Michigan's center for the Ku Klux Klan. There were several Black prisoners in my volunteer group, and I was more worried about citizens' reactions to them than any behavior the offenders might demonstrate. Fortunately for the program and me, the day went very well. Each offender stayed with his assigned resident, nobody reported any incidents, and everyone returned to camp at the end of the day. In fact, Hillcrest valued this program so highly that when I was promoted, they trained one of their staff to supervise offenders; he transported the prisoner volunteers until Hillcrest closed.

When I became Brighton's camp supervisor, I wondered about the response

I would get from my peers. Most of them had been with the agency more than ten years and had treated me like the camp mascot when I had attended the quarterly supervisor meetings during my first job. While in the Program Bureau, Deputy Director Kime and I presented the agency's new risk screening process and it was not very well received, although most were cordial to me. Now I was coming as an equal, even though we all knew I did not have the training or experience to function well as a camp supervisor. Since my nominal boss, the deputy superintendent, gave me no direction, I was hoping some of my fellow supervisors would help when I encountered things outside my limited experience.

That first meeting was interesting. Most of the supervisors were frosty. I knew John Andrews since Camp Waterloo was next door to Camp Control. He and Duane Corey, from Camp Lehman, were two who made a point of offering to be resources. In addition, they provided evening companionship. Our meetings were held at the McMullen Training Center, a rustic gathering place in a state park near Grayling. We stayed in rooms with bunk beds and the bath down the hall, although men and women did get separate accommodations. Evening entertainment usually involved some alcoholic beverages and snacks in a common area while swapping prison stories.

One of those evenings, Andrews and Corey decided we should take some beer and cruise the back roads looking for deer. It was Corey's territory, and deer season was approaching. They both lit up cigars, and, as the pickup cab filled with smoke, I recall asking for a cigar. "Gimme one of those. If I have to smell it, I might as well taste it too." To my amazement, I liked the taste and became a periodic cigar smoker, even though I abhorred cigarettes and did not allow smoking in the "pine box" at work. The cigar smoking would become a trademark. Before smoking was banned departmentwide, I would knit and smoke at meetings. The support of these two friends helped me through many early challenges. As I became more confident, Brighton staff came around, as did most of my peers. I recall a camp supervisors' meeting when John Hawley proclaimed, "Withrow, you're gonna make a hell of a corrections man someday." It felt like a blessing because John was known as an excellent supervisor. The fact that I would never be a man was lost in the sentiment of that time; gender was, and continued to be, an issue as I moved up in the department.

The next promotion came about, I think, as a result of an unscheduled visit by the director, Perry Johnson, and one of his deputy directors (and my former boss), Bill Kime. They were returning from business in the Detroit area, had a little extra time, and decided to stop at Camp Brighton to see how things were going. Well, having the director visit was a big deal! Fortunately for me, the camp was in great shape. Hugh Leemon was the regular officer on days at the time. He had drawn up and posted detailed descriptions for every job a prisoner did at the camp. For example, the directions for a porter washing walls began with "get a bucket," and continued with water temperature, type of cleaning supplies to use for scrubbing, and even that walls should be washed from the bottom to prevent streaking. This level of detail clearly impressed the director. He also seemed to like the fact that the facility was clean and orderly, that staff treated me with respect, and the prisoners were not surprised to see me move around the camp. I told him and Deputy Director Kime that I took count, conducted pat shakedowns as needed, and usually transported disruptive prisoners or those needing medical care to Jackson, since that was considered more desirable than leaving me alone in the camp. Our staffing pattern occasionally left me as the second "officer" for the day. If the lieutenant was visiting Work Pass or DNR assignments, I would back up the assigned officer. Learning basic security skills was useful as I assessed the performance of staff later in my career. Of course, I had a chance to tell a story or two as we shared coffee after our tour. I told our visitors about a Work Pass participant who had recently been a victim of crime. This man had literacy limitations, so another prisoner had offered to help him complete his application for a savings account at a local bank. When his monthly statement came, the prisoner looked to his earlier helper to assist him in deciphering it. Apparently, the helper had also noted the account number and, when released, had wiped out the balance of the victim's account. Naturally, the defrauded prisoner wanted to complain to the police, so we assisted him in contacting the state police and making his complaint. I took him to court the day his case was to be heard. He had to take the day off work to appear. Imagine the complaining prisoner's dismay when the defendant's attorney asked for a continuance due to his client's work schedule! He ranted about the unfairness of the system and was feeling quite sorry for himself, since he would have to take another day off work without pay when the next hearing rolled around. I did not comment on his situation other than asking, "Did you and your attorney ever play that game when you were charged with crimes?" He stopped complaining to me after that.

Another interesting prisoner was an older man in prison for property crimes. We permitted families to bring in picnic lunches on Sundays during the summer when visits were outdoors. We noticed that this man was visited by his girlfriend and her children, who he stated were also his, on Saturday, and then by his wife and an older set of children on Sunday. If all the children had lined up together, they would have numbered about a dozen, with not much over a year between each. We asked the prisoner how he managed to keep his wife from coming up on Saturday and discovering his girlfriend. He said they knew about each other and were friendly. His wife just got old, he said, and he wanted someone younger; his wife wanted to stay married, so this was how they worked things out.

Probably the most poignant story I can recall is the offender who asked to meet with me in my office. He was very emotional and said he had a personal issue to discuss. He said his wife was pregnant. I knew he had been in prison long enough that the baby was not his and he acknowledged that; however, he said his issue was really with his family. They were pressuring him to divorce his wife. He said, with remarkable empathy, that it was not his wife's fault that he was in prison and he had been down a long time. She was a young woman and he understood how she could have gotten involved. He further stated that he loved babies, thought he and his wife could be good parents to this baby, and he wanted her to have it. He wanted to stay married and be a family. I did not have any words of wisdom for this man; he was in uncharted territory in my experience. I thought then, and still believe, that he was able to have that conversation with me because I was a woman. He knew most of the male staff would echo his family's advice—throw her out—and he thought, correctly, that I would just listen and let him work out the problem for himself. That experience was one that affirmed for me the value of having staff of both genders as resources for prisoners.

»»»»»»»»»»»»

It was lonely being the only woman at Camp Brighton and I was delighted to hear from Luella Burke, who had replaced me in the Program Bureau. She had met Tekla Miller, who had a friend from the Field Services part of the agency, Denise Quarles. Luella was an early networking fan and thought the four of us should meet for lunch in Lansing. At this point, I was ready for some time away from the camp and really ready for time with other women, so I readily agreed. We hit it off from the beginning and even talked of traveling together to the American Correctional Association Conference that would be held in Toronto in August of 1982. That was still over a year off but gave me something to look forward to and save up for.

After the second lieutenant left, I finally promoted the surly sergeant. Staff were delighted that one of their own was now in charge. Mike Meader became sergeant and completed his BA in time to be eligible for an added resident unit manager position, which also supervised the afternoon shift. The night shift corporal became the night shift sergeant when the corporal position was abolished. I now had in place an excellent cadre of supervisors, and this was complemented by a stable group of experienced officers. Then we got the news that we would be getting a recreation director. Ordinarily, I would have been delighted with this news. Lt. Rupp had been handling most things related to the gym, and, given his security background, that mostly meant he climbed a tree adjacent to the window of the room containing the pool table and came swinging down when he saw tokens on the table to bust everyone involved for gambling.

The reason we were getting a recreation director was that Camp Pontiac was being converted to house women; no male staff would remain there. (As an aside, my new friend Tekla would be the supervisor of the new camp, renamed Camp Gilman.) Most camps did not have a recreation director. The only reason Camp Pontiac had one was that our new employee had failed as a camp supervisor, but, for some reason, the agency did not want to terminate him. Instead, they placed another man over him. That meant, in civil-service terms, that they had a twenty-five-level running that camp. Regular camp supervisors were civil-service grade twelve, and the incompetent's supervisor had to be a grade thirteen to outrank him, thus the joke that Pontiac had a "twenty-five" running it. There was not much enthusiasm about this addition to our ranks, but he needed an office, so I put the lieutenant in charge of locating and outfitting it.

On the day the recreation director was to arrive, I was working a late shift and arrived about 10:00 a.m. The new employee was in his car in the parking lot. He rolled down his window a crack and hissed at me, "I will put in my papers to retire this afternoon." Not waiting for a reply, he left, spraying gravel all over the lot. I went into the office and found the staff convulsed with laughter. "Alright, what happened?" I recall asking. Wordlessly, the lieutenant beckoned me to follow him to the gym. He opened the door to the rec director's office. What had been a small equipment room had been painted electric blue and was nearly filled with a desk painted Kelly green. The floor was covered with splotches of both colors. A bare light bulb with a pull chain illuminated this awful spectacle. My lieutenant had succeeded where the corrections bureaucracy had failed for years. The incompetent would no longer receive a regular paycheck from Corrections.

»»»»»»»»»»»»

To prepare me for additional responsibility, Director Johnson sent me to the American Institute of Justice's Workshop on Prisoner Discipline in Toledo, Ohio. Participants were from Michigan and adjacent states and the course material was interesting. The US Supreme Court had begun to rethink their hands-off approach to prisons and had ruled, several years earlier, that prisoners had due process rights. While it had taken a while, corrections agencies nationwide were now implementing rules and processes for handling prisoner misconduct and sanctions. The workshop highlighted the challenging changes agencies faced.

Like many other corrections gatherings, evenings involved quantities of alcohol. One night, the bar featured Ladies' Night—drinks were two for one. I thought I could keep up with the guys but miscalculated. While I made it to my room, I stripped and fell into bed without pajamas. This was a time when deaths in hotel fires had received extensive publicity. When my alarm went off, my alcohol-fogged brain registered the noise as a fire alarm. In a panic, I wrapped a sheet around my body and exited into the hall. There I found fellow workshop attendees on their way to breakfast. Oops. I sobered up quickly, but my door had closed and locked and there was no pocket in the sheet for a key. I knocked on the door of the adjacent room and the occupant let me use his phone to call the desk. When the bellman arrived, with as much dignity as I could muster, I told him that I seemed to have misplaced my key and needed to get into my room. Without comment, he unlocked my door.

In corrections, you meet your responsibilities, even with a massive hangover; I showered, dressed, grabbed coffee and a roll, then headed to class. Apparently, no one reported my indiscreet behavior, although some of my classmates were from Michigan because, not long after that training, I was offered a promotion. That was ironic, since Brighton now had the best group of supervisors and officers than at any time in my tenure and I was not going to be able to enjoy it. To add to the irony, the promotion was to Jackson, which had just experienced a major disturbance. While I had always asked to be a camp supervisor, my taste of Jackson during the officer training evaluation meant that place was never on my list of places to work. However, when you have been given your first choice and enjoyed that, you swallow and accept your last.

»»»»»»»»»»»

Lesson Learned: When you want to try something new, call it a pilot project and set a time limit. In the press of business, it is likely no one will think to follow up on the outcome.

Corrections Story: One of the Work Pass assignments was in the restaurant at the Holiday Inn in Howell. That was always a concern, since alcohol was served and the freeway was nearby, creating a double threat—drinking and escape. Because of these concerns, staff made frequent stops at the site. One day, the prisoner was not on his kitchen assignment when staff showed up. It turned out that the restaurant found it was short staffed and had started letting the prisoner deliver room-service meals. Once that practice started, the prisoner informed his wife of his new duties and she rented a room, so he delivered meals and more! He was especially sad when his Work Pass job ended.

5. JACKSON

A prison riot is akin to a tornado in a small town. There is significant injury, destruction of property, and, occasionally, a miraculous escape from harm. The comparison breaks down when the review of a riot is completed. Inevitably, it turns out that all the terror, injury, and loss of property resulted from poor decisions. Jackson's events ignited the riots at the Reformatory and Marquette; consequently, Jackson was the focus of the investigation into the riots' cause.

The 1981 Memorial Day weekend prison disturbances in Michigan resulted from a breakdown of the three-legged stool of prison management. One leg is prisoner needs; one is staff needs; the final leg is the combined needs of prison administrators and external forces (laws, policy, politics, community concerns, the media, and Central Office). A warden must keep all these legs proportionate or the prison gets out of balance and, like a stool with a short leg, comes crashing down.

At the State Prison of Southern Michigan (commonly called Jackson), corrections officers, through their union, had raised concerns about the proliferation of prison-made weapons. They demanded that the high-security Central Complex be locked down for a general shakedown. When the warden refused, the officers locked down without authorization and conducted their shakedown at the beginning of the Memorial Day holiday weekend. Not surprisingly, this alarmed the prisoners, who count on the administration to keep staff under control. When prisoners were finally released for routine activities, they refused to return to their cells and began destroying any state property they could find. Adding to the confusion was a planned changeover in the internal phone system, which disrupted communication. The deputy in charge for the holiday weekend was in the medium-security North Complex. He was able to gain only limited information about what was happening in Central Complex and was unable to contact the warden to alert him to the situation or ask for direction.

The media somehow found out and began converging on Jackson. Custody staff were trying to control the rampaging prisoners and did not pay any attention to the TV cameras outside the perimeter filming the smoke coming from inside the prison. The warden first knew of the riot from media reports. The Reformatory was the first prison to imitate Jackson. Then, although all of Jackson's prisoners had been locked down, North Complex prisoners were released prematurely and began destroying their part of the prison. That ignited a riot at Marquette. Events in the department went downhill from there, with plenty of poor decisions to keep investigators busy for months. The immediate concern at Jackson was to figure out how to rebuild trust between the officers and administrators while developing a new way of operating that would avoid a repeat of riots.

It is a truth in the corrections business that a riot will result in staff changes. Often the warden will be fired or forced to retire. Other key administrators will be reassigned or replaced. It was not surprising, then, that not long after the riot, I received a call that turned my life upside down. The call directed me to move from idyllic Camp Brighton to Jackson, the world's largest walled prison. As the warden's administrative assistant, I would be responsible for media relations, answering prisoner grievances, and responding to correspondence for the warden. As a result of the riot, I would also be sitting through interminable meetings as we determined what the new normal would be at this troubled facility. It was still locked down. Prisoners were being fed in their cells and prisoner movement was permitted only for visits and medical emergencies. Even the right to do legal work was accommodated by the delivery of materials to prisoners' cells rather than risking out-of-cell movement.

When I arrived, staff were still reeling from the interpersonal violence they had seen. Fires had destroyed Prison Industries. While some staff offices in the cellblocks were trashed or burned, others were spared. In the same vein, some staff had been protected by prisoners while others had to seek refuge in the catwalks (utility corridors behind prisoner cells). The latter had suffered from the heat and smoke until they could be rescued. Prisoners who had grievances against each other used broomsticks and other homemade weapons to even old scores. Those thought to be snitches and the weak were victimized. Even though the prison was not under staff control for many hours, there was no loss of life; however, property damage was extensive. In the end, the concrete and steel construction prevailed; no escapes resulted during the confusion.

As the warden's representative, I needed to appear competent and in control. This was difficult because I knew little about how this, or any other penitentiary, operated. It was true that I had attended new officers' school at Jackson, but I did not work as an officer inside the secure perimeter, so was unfamiliar with daily operations and the physical plant. Fortunately, good staff came to my aid. Charley Anderson, who had once served as Jackson's warden, told me that people would try to make an issue of my gender and that I should let that be their problem. As one of the early Black appointees in corrections, he certainly had the perspective to offer that advice. Later, when I became assistant deputy warden for housing in Central Complex, the man I was replacing patiently went through the responsibilities of the position. He noted that many of the tasks he had been charged with were not really his job; they had just been piled on because administrators were trying to get rid of him. He suggested that I discard these as quickly as possible. That was a kind action on his part, and I was touched that he had the integrity to help me during a time of personal disgrace. Later, I realized that his move to Trustee Division, the minimum-security part of Jackson, improved his quality of life immeasurably, and that I had inherited a really awful job.

Before moving into that next job, I had three months of working for the warden. We all understood that he and other key staff were unlikely to remain, since he would be held responsible for the riot. He and his staff, however, went on with their duties as if there were no sword hanging over their heads. Because the facility was in such disarray, the media and legislators were not initially permitted inside. Instead, they (and I) had to climb a ladder five levels to the roof to survey the damage. Armed posts were also accessed from this route; weapons might be used from any vantage point, so barriers were not in the interest of good security. There were low railings at the roof's edge to offer a handhold in case someone fell during inclement weather. I had never had any problem with heights and took malicious glee in leading wary legislators and media representatives to the roof's edge as I pointed out the various structures damaged by rampaging prisoners. The prisoner store was a target since food and OTC medications were stored there. It was harder to understand the wanton destruction of other areas, especially Prison Industries, where the most desirable prisoner jobs were located.

I had barely become familiar with my first position when I was promoted to be the assistant deputy warden (ADW) for housing in Central Complex. The new job involved overseeing seven cell blocks housing 2,800 prisoners. One of those units, Five Block, was for segregation and detention (a jail within the prison) and the other, half of Seven Block, for protection (a place for prisoners fearful for their safety or for whom staff felt needed protection from other prisoners). While officer scheduling was handled by the shift commander, I supervised the seven resident unit managers (RUMs) and their assistants (the counseling staff) as well as the housing secretary. As I got to know those staff,

I came to understand why only some of the staff offices were destroyed. Each RUM and their two assistants were responsible for about three times as many prisoners as I had managed at Camp Brighton. Not surprisingly, some were burned out and cynical. Others, however, managed to remain professional and get their jobs done well. In my case, policy said I needed to visit all housing units daily. In addition, there were transfers to write, security classification hearings to oversee, grievances to investigate, prisoner kites (letters) to read, too many meetings, and, of course, any additional tasks the deputy assigned.

Getting work done was hampered by the fact that there were no bathroom facilities for women inside the prison. The deputy had a private bathroom in his office, which he would let the women use except when his door was closed. That was a signal to stay out. Traversing the security gates to and from the public restroom took nearly half an hour. Given that Jackson ran on coffee, multiple daily trips were needed. The women in the area considered me a hero when I managed to get a mop closet converted to a restroom. Those issues aside, I was drowning. Nothing at Brighton had prepared me for the crushing workload at Jackson. I knew I needed to follow policy, but signing logbooks in all seven cell blocks, making even a cursory inspection of each, and talking with staff was a full day! I would work late to catch up on office duties. Not surprisingly, my personal life was suffering badly.

In despair, I went to Director Johnson and explained that I was not up to the job and wanted to return to Camp Brighton. He responded, "Don't worry about it, sis; nobody's ever been able to do that job. Just do your best." I went back and gave it my best for a couple more weeks. No improvement. I tried again to convince the director that I was just not cut out for Jackson's workload. Out of frustration, I even cried, something I had never done at work. Perry again told me, less gently, that I needed to continue to do my best and sent me back to hell.

In addition to feeling like I was failing at work, my personal life was deteriorating. While I was still at Brighton, the bus driver and I had decided to build a house from a kit and had that nearly completed when I started at Jackson. He had been promoted to training director for the Capitol Area Transportation Authority and had the stress of a new job. In addition, we had moved two children from his previous marriage into our lives. The boy, older than John, was not biologically my husband's; however, the boy's mother was unable to care for him. His daughter, youngest of the three, was confused by the move and resentful. Our life was chaos with two working parents, one of whom was not present very much. My son, John, survived by spending much of his free time with his buddy, Jim Christie, who lived nearby, and my parents, who lived within walking distance.

The older boy had emotional issues which resulted in destructive behavior such as smashing or spray painting all the Christmas gifts of the other two children. When his mother demanded that he be returned to her, we all breathed a sigh of relief. However, we resisted the daughter's return. The mother's history of instability did not bode well for a young girl's long-term development; however, the fates intervened. While my husband had been supportive of my career initially, three promotions in five years had me making more money than he did and working crazy hours to survive. The marriage was in trouble, and those two doomed children were victims of our inability to work through our problems. John and I moved into an apartment in Haslett, and I began to plot my escape from Jackson.

That plan involved a move out of state. A bit of history is needed here. As part of his vision to integrate women into management positions in the department, Perry Johnson had sent many of us to training at the National Academy of Corrections in Colorado. I had loved the courses, and learned a lot from peers from around the country as well as the instructors who were seasoned correctional administrators on leave from their agencies for two years. I had become friends with the staff at the academy and expressed an interest in returning to teach once I had the requisite experience. The director of the academy was supportive of that plan and encouraged me to apply. I did. Perry signed off on the application and I waited for a response. In the meantime, I kept working crazy, exhausting hours, and failing in my duties as a parent. Fortunately, John, a freshman at Haslett High, was independent and resourceful, and my parents, again, served as local support when I was unable to be present.

Another survival strategy was to call on my gal pals. Luella Burke had become a friend when she came into the Camp Program when I left the first time and then followed me into the Program Bureau when I was promoted to Camp Brighton. Denise Quarles and Tekla Miller were friends from the Field Services part of Corrections. We got together while Luella was in the Program Bureau. Then Tekla became the supervisor of Camp Gilman, which had been converted to a camp for women prisoners. We had bonded over our experiences as pioneer women in corrections and continued to get together monthly while I was at Jackson. Denise was running a corrections center in Detroit at that point. I do not think I would have made it out of there with my sanity without the help of those three. We would meet, talk, laugh, and strategize. Stories of who would help and who was dangerous were shared. When someone suggested we travel by train to the American Correctional Association's conference in Toronto, it was easy to say yes. Denise and Tekla stayed at the downtown hotel near the conference headquarters. Luella and I, financially challenged, stayed in university housing some distance from the action, but we met up for all the conference functions and had a great time. And we became friends for life.

Although we adopted the appellation, others first called us the "Network." We liked the name and continue to refer to our group that way to this day.

»»»»»»»»»»»

Over time, I acknowledged I could not do all that policy required and simply did what I thought was most important. Jackson was recovering from the riot, and prisoners were able to move about more freely. As a result, assaults increased. Four Block was the most troublesome. I had been discussing the assault problem with one of the officers and tasked him to come up with a plan to reduce violence. He managed to do that, although assaults on the yard went up. I later found out that the officer had enlisted the help of a prisoner nicknamed Nine Lives—for the nine life sentences for contract killings he had committed—who had advised his fellow prisoners that Four Block was not the place for assaults. Unfortunately, I had promoted the officer to sergeant before learning of his inappropriate use of a prisoner enforcer to get the violence stopped.

Assaults in the yard were not my problem since the custody ADW was responsible for that area. He and I were competitors for promotion, but also locked into roles that required we cooperate to get back to full operation without a repeat of the violence that was always threatening. As the anniversary of the riot approached, staff in the prison held their breath. I made rounds, talked with staff and prisoners, tried to balance the need for prisoner movement with safety/security concerns, and continued to work way too many hours.

It was during one of those late nights in the summer that staff reported that we had a problem on the yard. A fight had broken out and an officer in a tower had shot into the yard. He hit a prisoner wearing kitchen whites, so blood from the leg wound was startlingly vivid. Since that prisoner had not been involved in the fight, there was muttering about staff wrongdoing. Prisoners were milling about in unusual patterns and some seemed to be trying to stir up others. Staff who usually patrolled the yard were removed to relative safety outside the fenced recreation area. Staff in Three and Four Blocks, whose prisoners were on the yard, locked their unit doors. Prisoners who wanted to get out of the escalating tension had nowhere to go, which further agitated them. As is often the case in these situations, information was hard to come by and conflicting. I was the highest ranking official on duty, so went to the yard to see and hear what was happening. All the walking and talking I had been doing paid off. Staff and prisoners were willing to tell me what was happening from their perspective. The issue of locked unit doors was quickly identified as the most important thing to remedy. Since I supervised housing, the officers responded, reluctantly, to my order to open the doors and begin admitting prisoners. Many took this opportunity to go lock up.

I promised the prisoners who were concerned about the wounded inmate that I would find out why he was shot. At the same time, I intimated that Warden Foltz was on his way to the facility. Dale Foltz, a former Michigan State University football star who cut an imposing figure, had replaced my initial boss. He had made it clear that he was not going to put up with any prisoner foolishness. There was a rumor that the arsenal included Thompson submachine guns and I did nothing to discourage the belief that Warden Foltz would put those to work if things got out of hand. The rest of the prisoners wisely decided to lock up. I called the warden to tell him we had a shot fired on the yard and an injured prisoner, but the situation was under control and he need not come to the prison. When we interviewed the officer who had shot the prisoner, he admitted that he targeted the prisoner with the white uniform because he had a clear shot in the evening light. The officer was charged with excessive use of force. This was not a popular decision, since staff felt any use of force to curtail prisoner violence on the yard was appropriate. After that night, they understood that shooting an uninvolved prisoner was not okay.

This leads me to another situation where staff seemed to forget it was their job to protect prisoners. An inmate in segregation with the nickname Lucky was in a closed-front cell because of his continued poor behavior. I happened to walk into the unit and saw smoke coming from the bottom of the door. When I asked what was going on, staff said, without much interest, that Lucky had set paper in his cell on fire. I ordered them to get him out promptly. While they did so and took him to the infirmary to be checked out for smoke inhalation, they seemed to share the opinion that he would have learned more had he been left to choke on the smoke a little longer.

Five Block segregation was the setting for my only encounter with a prisoner where I was genuinely fearful—even though the inmate was behind bars and could not get to me. He had been convicted of a single murder committed in 1970, but was the suspect in multiple murders of young women in the Ann Arbor area in the late 1960s. Although convicted under the name John Norman Collins, he adopted a different name for serving his sentence. He was a Canadian citizen, and there was an agreement between the US and Canada that their citizens could serve their prison sentences in their home country if both jurisdictions agreed. Collins's family had started the legal process for the transfer, and all was going smoothly until the deputy director for prisons, Robert Brown Jr., was asked to sign routine paperwork to finalize the move. Bob Brown had an amazing ability to recall troublemakers and notorious offenders housed in his prisons. He knew of Collins's name change. He immediately realized that the natural life sentence (life with no possibility of parole) Collins was serving in Michigan would not be in effect in Canada. He would be eligible for parole in twenty years under their laws. Brown knew Collins was dangerous and should never rejoin the free community. Also, the families of the murdered women would feel betrayed if this prisoner failed to serve his entire life behind bars. Deputy Director Brown nixed the deal, and I was sent to advise the prisoner that he was staying in Michigan. The conversation started pleasantly when I told Collins that I was there to discuss his transfer to Canada. His mask of affability shifted when I explained that Michigan would not agree to such a transfer and he would be staying with us. The look he gave me made it clear that, absent those bars, he would have wrung my neck. I had never seen such naked and feral hatred in my life. Believing the prisoner was not likely to forget this encounter, I took advantage of the special problem offender process and had a notice placed in his file prohibiting him from being housed in a prison where I worked; I then initiated his transfer out of Jackson.

Another prisoner I recall from Jackson brings happier memories. As I made rounds, I kept noticing an exceptionally large and not handsome Black man who wore pink foam rollers in his hair. Those rollers were not sold in the prisoner store or part of the barbershop's inventory, so I was curious enough to ask the prisoner's unit officer to enlighten me. The officer was an old hand who explained matter-of-factly that the prisoner was doing life on the installment plan (in and out of prison for short sentences) and that, while he had a wife and kids on the street, he had adopted the role of passive homosexual in prison. It suited him to keep house for a stronger prisoner who would protect him and provide amenities in exchange for services. In addition to sex, he would clean the other fellow's cell and do his laundry. Oh my, the things you learn in prison.

I also ran across a former Brighton resident inside Jackson. Since the man had done well in minimum security, I asked him what he was doing inside a high-security place. Well, he had committed one too many crimes in his home community. He now had a K prefix before his six-digit prison number. Prisoners start at the beginning of the alphabet and get letters sequentially each time they return to prison with a new sentence, so he did have quite a history. The local prosecutor had decided to charge him as a habitual offender, which resulted in a sentence long enough that he was ineligible for minimum security for several more years. This encounter made me realize that we needed more long-term low-security prisons because the cost of housing this innocuous character in high security was punishing the taxpayers as well as the offender.

Another memorable prisoner event occurred in Six Block. Whenever I was working late and a prisoner refused to move from his cell, I asked for a chance to talk with him before we sent in a squad for a forced move. Staff had to notify me in any case because they could not administer chemical agents without the approval of someone at my level or higher. Most of the time, I was able to reason with the prisoner and he moved without incident. This reduced the chance of prisoner or staff injury. It also cut down on cleaning costs for the body armor that staff wore. I thought all these reasons were worth my time and attention. On this occasion, however, the prisoner was not going anywhere voluntarily.

Six Block was a unit with cells around the outside of the block, so five tiers of cells housing over two hundred inmates overlooked the area where this prisoner was showboating. Also, the unit was built later in the prison construction process; as a result, the cell doors were sometimes able to be opened by the prisoners if they gave a sharp jerk on the door. This was understandably a concern in a tense situation. The shift captain was commanding the squad. The prisoner started to light a cigarette just before I gave the order to deploy the chemical agent. I paused to confirm with the captain that the gas was not flammable. He said it was not. I gave the order to go in, gas was dispersed, and the prisoner's head was surrounded by flame. The prisoners watching the action roared in outrage. I told the captain, "Get that guy out so we can go now." The prisoner was so startled that he did not put up a fight. He was cuffed and carried out of the unit in record time, while the officers in the block were left to clean up the debris thrown by the witnesses to the flames. Fortunately for the prisoner, the fire did little damage. He looked like he had a mild sunburn with some loss of lashes and eyebrows. Apparently, no one above me read the incident report closely because there were no repercussions. The prisoner did not even sue. I, however, had a stern chat with the captain. "I thought you said the gas wasn't flammable." He stuttered in response, "I was right, Dep. The gas wasn't flammable, but the propellant was." Small distinctions.

The last memorable incident was a murder in one of the honor blocks. Eleven and Twelve Blocks were reserved for prisoners who stayed free of misconduct and held jobs. As Jackson recovered from the riot, fencing had been erected to control prisoner movement and keep groups of prisoners apart. Despite the efforts to restrict contact, the prison subculture flourished.

Four Block, with the most violent general population prisoners, evolved into a home for the enforcers. Three, Six, and Eight Blocks housed those who used the goods and services provided by the movers and shakers, who lived in the honor blocks. The incident was the last of three murders which occurred while I was at Jackson. The first was because a prisoner had stolen another's coat and would not pay for it when confronted; the second resulted from a problem on the street. The reason for the last one was not discovered as the perpetrator was never identified. I believe it had to do with a struggle for control of one of the many schemes and scams run out of the supposed honor blocks.

»»»»»»»»»»»»

Around Christmas 1982, I got an early gift. The Corrections Academy in Colorado had an opening; it was mine if I wanted it. Did I ever! I contacted the director's office to arrange a release date. I was leaving Jackson. John had developed a taste for skiing after a trip to the Rockies with his Aunt Chere and Uncle Mike and was delighted at the prospect of a couple years near the mountains. We were both giddy at the prospect of this move. Then Perry called back: "Something's come up, sis. I can't talk about it now, but you can't go to the academy." I now understood how a prisoner felt when his parole was revoked. But you do not argue with the head guy. I continued soldiering on at Jackson, but with a bitterness I did not know I could muster. Perry had been my godfather in the department, and I had prospered as a result. Now it seemed he had abandoned me to the horrors of Jackson; I was bereft. Almost as painful, I had to tell John that our move was off. I also had to advise academy staff that, while I had wanted to come, something had come up to prevent the assignment at this time, but to please keep me in mind.

It was less than a month later that I found out what that "something" was; I was going to be the superintendent at the Michigan Dunes Correctional Facility. This was the first time in our state that a woman would head a prison housing adult male felons. I was making history, but more important to me at the time was that I was finally getting out of Jackson! Though not without a party. Staff in Housing decided that I had been a tolerably good ADW, and they wanted to give me a send-off. They planned a nice event at the local Holiday Inn, and I invited my son, parents, Director Johnson, and his wife, Uyvonne. The evening was going along nicely when the Five Block officers came up with their huge, boxed present. Things got kind of quiet, and I guessed that I was about to be pranked. Was I ever! The gift was in honor of my newly single status—a full-size, male, anatomically correct, blow-up doll. Horrors! Fortunately, I did not remove it completely from the box; unfortunately, many there had previewed the gift and were clear about the anatomically correct part and made raucous comments. I think my family, Perry, and his wife tried to ignore them. I was quite embarrassed, which, no doubt, was the point of the gift.

In corrections we do not let anything go to waste; so that doll made the circuit of the Network women in celebration of birthdays, anniversaries, or any other event we could make up to move the awful thing on to someone else. I am not sure who had it last, but it stopped surfacing, so it must have been thrown out. I remember Denise saying once, "What do I say to the cleaning lady if she finds it?" We had a good laugh over that one.

»»»»»»»»»»»

Lesson Learned: While policies provide a framework, it is sometimes necessary to meet the intent of these to the best of your ability with the resources available. Letting your boss know about your concerns is a good idea, too.

Corrections Story: The first warden I worked for at Jackson liked to take his subordinates out to lunch. One day, I complained about the housework and laundry piling up at home. With a grin, he said, "Withrow, what you need is a wife!" That got a laugh from the others in the vehicle.

6. THE MICHIGAN DUNES CORRECTIONAL FACILITY

On Valentine's Day 1983, I woke as the first woman warden of a male prison in Michigan. Both excited and scared, I knew Director Perry Johnson would do all he could to help me succeed, as would Deputy Director Robert Brown Jr. I also knew that there would be people actively working against me, and others hoping I would fail. The network of corrections women (now dear friends) would be supporters, as would some former coworkers and members of the Michigan Corrections Association. I also joined the North American Association of Wardens and Superintendents (NAAWS) because I knew learning from a national network of peers would be critical to survival. Having gone to an American Correctional Association conference while at Jackson, I planned to find funds to continue to attend for professional development and new ideas.

In the meantime, I had a prison to run, but no permanent place to live. The facility's address was Holland, and that was where I first sought an apartment. John and I had spent three days in January touring the area and visiting Holland High School. Curiously, the local newspaper had no listing for rentals. I inquired and was directed to a landlord consortium. Given a form to complete, I answered the usual questions about employment and income. However, the remaining queries were about religious affiliation, smoking, drinking, and drug use. There was a reason the rentals were not advertised; a number of those questions were not legal. Consequently, I looked elsewhere. The town south of the prison, Saugatuck, was a resort community with rentals beyond my means, so that was not an option.

Until I could find a permanent place, I stayed in a furnished apartment at the Robins Nest on the shores of Holland's Lake Macatawa. Somehow, I needed to find affordable housing that would feel like home for John and me. Ultimately, I did find an apartment only seven miles from the prison in Ganges and moved there in March. John wanted to finish his freshman year at Haslett High; because I could not change my lease, family again came to my rescue. My youngest sister, nineteen-year-old Kristy, moved into the apartment with John until school was out. I was lonely, but John's absence did give me time to focus on the responsibilities inherent in managing the Dunes, getting to know staff, and learning the facility operations and physical plant. John joined me that summer and we settled in our new home.

The departing warden said he would show me the ropes; however, even while we were sharing an office, he continued to handle the work without discussing it with me. As in the past, I learned the job by doing it. One source of support was Kathi Kars, the warden's secretary, who was a font of knowledge willing to advise me when reports were due and how various activities had been handled in the past. Most department heads were cooperative and helpful; the deputy warden was not.

Other wardens proved willing to offer advice and direction. Director Johnson arranged for me to attend the West Central Wardens' conference in Minneapolis in May. I traveled with three seasoned wardens: Dale Foltz, Jackson; Steve Handlon, Michigan Training Unit; and Gary Wells, Muskegon. I listened to their prison stories as we drove roundtrip. We attended workshops, and I toured Minnesota's high-security prison. In those days, new wardens brought a half gallon of J&B scotch to their first wardens' meeting; partying was part of the culture. Wanting desperately to fit in, I drank heavily but never missed a meeting or time at work due to alcohol consumption.

As soon as I arrived at the Dunes, the media inquiries rolled in. I handled these with much more skill than at Brighton and survived the rounds of interviews and photographs. Having worked in the warden's office at Jackson, I had some idea of the duties; however, I failed to appreciate how much power came with the job. The previous warden had a large desk, which I liked; however, his large chair just did not fit my petite frame, so I sent it away, mentioning that I preferred the wooden chair I had brought from Jackson, but that it looked pretty beat up for the nice office I had inherited. The next day, that chair was gone! I asked my secretary about it, and she said she had sent it to the building trades shop for refinishing. I quickly learned not to muse aloud.

As is often the case for newly appointed wardens, I had to deal with a disappointed deputy who had interviewed for the job. He made no bones about his dissatisfaction with affirmative action appointments, but was professional enough not to be disrespectful to my face. In an agency that traditionally had valued years of progressive responsibilities, my promotion to warden with under seven years' experience was irregular. That I had been an assistant deputy for only sixteen months and never held a deputy's position were also marks against me. Staff later told me that the deputy had made it clear they had to choose between him or me because he planned to run me out.

On the plus side, the facility was running like a Swiss watch. My predecessor was a no-nonsense guy who had ensured his staff were familiar with policy and procedure and that the prison operated within those guidelines. It was a conversion prison. Formerly a Catholic seminary, it was not built with security in mind. However, it was beautiful, with a curving central hall and lots of windows in the library and classrooms. The dining room was built like the prow of a ship and had huge windows overlooking the dune for which the place was named. That dune also blocked the view of Lake Michigan just to the west. Other wardens joked that I had the only joint with marble mopboards.

The community had been adamantly opposed to the prison—to the point of hanging Director Perry Johnson in effigy at a public hearing. Therefore, various concessions had been made about the characteristics of prisoners housed there. Effectively, the prisoners were the type I had at Camp Brighton except with longer sentences. When I arrived, there were 328 beds for Level II prisoners (low-medium custody designation), slightly more than twice the number at Brighton and a far cry from the 2,800 I had been responsible for at Jackson.

»»»»»»»»»»»»

This might be a good time to mention that I have always thought of a prison as a small town, with all the services one might expect to find there. Most staff are responsible for security, operating like a police force. In fact, some prisoners call them the PO-lice. There is also a need for food service, laundry, a quartermaster, maintenance, transportation, a library, a school, a chapel, counseling, healthcare, a barber shop, a store, a warehouse, and even a jail. In addition, administrative services, business, records, personnel, and additional maintenance and warehouse space are outside the security perimeter.

Except for security, prisoners perform most of the work inside prisons. Although staff oversee food service, prisoners make the food, serve it, and perform cleanup chores. Prisoner clerks assist with the library, school, chapel, and quartermaster. A barber in the free world in Michigan could not get a license with a felony conviction, yet prisoners cut hair in institutions. They also clean, mow, shovel snow, make repairs, and operate the commissary with staff supervision. Staff costs are a prison's largest budget item. Prisoner wages, at that time, were under a dollar a day for most jobs. Their labor saved the taxpayers significant operational costs.

»»»»»»»»»»»

A common misperception is that staff carry a weapon inside a prison. The fact is that the primary tool used by staff is their brain. Prisoners have twenty-four hours a day to dream up ways to beat the systems we have developed, and staff must stay on their toes to prevent and detect rule violations, especially escapes or disturbances. Most disciplinary matters are handled internally; however, felonies committed in Michigan's prisons are referred to the state police, with prosecutions handled by the county. Fortunately, the Dunes had few problems requiring outside help. While many prisoners did not like the large dormitory housing units, the prospect of living in the honor dorm or one of the eight single-man rooms was incentive for good behavior.

The arsenal contained restraints, rifles, shotguns, handguns, and chemical agents. These were assigned to perimeter and prisoner transport vehicles, used during annual weapons qualifications and for riot training. Fortunately, at the Dunes, there was never a call to use them for a disturbance.

However, I did create a question for an assistant deputy interview that involved use of force during a nonviolent prisoner sit-down strike on the yard. In the scenario, the candidates would have to decide whether to relay the order for squad members to shoot passive prisoners. An additional caveat was that the deputy issuing the order appeared to be intoxicated. To my amazement, over half of the candidates said they would give the order to shoot. I sent follow-up letters to those who had said they would give the order, reminding them that the policy governing use of deadly force permits it only if there is a clear and present danger, and that following orders issued by an inebriated person is not defensible even if that person is your boss. I suggested that they brush up on that policy. One recipient, still convinced he was right to follow orders even if it was a policy violation, took the time to write and tell me so. My memory is that no one else promoted him either.

As often happens when a warden leaves, some of the staff are tapped to work at the departing warden's new prison. That was how I found myself with an assistant deputy vacancy and hired Carol Howes. Like me, Carol had worked in the Program Bureau. Before that, she had worked for the legislature; her background was broader than most in the DOC, but she lacked prison experience. The Dunes was a good place to gain that experience;

additionally, I knew Carol had the moxie to contain the deputy's sometimes counterproductive initiatives. As in my case, he urged staff to run her out, but she was an excellent employee and won over the security staff who worked for her as well as others at the prison. She was a good listener and modeled the professionalism I wanted all to embrace.

Because Director Johnson had sent me to the National Academy of Corrections for two- and four-week training sessions in leadership and management, I knew how valuable that experience was for prison managers without the usual on-the-job experience. Thus, I sent Carol off to Colorado; she reported that it gave her many of the tools she needed, especially for managing her difficult boss.

There were not many incidents at this low-security prison. However, we did have a prisoner death—a nice man who had been the painter for the facility. Although the death appeared to be from natural causes, the prison doctor ordered an autopsy for confirmation. Just as I had qualified with the rifle, shotgun, and handgun at Jackson so that I would understand the process, I was determined to attend the autopsy. If I were going to send staff to observe these in the future, I wanted to know what they would experience. I recall the doctor performing the procedure looking at our prison physician and asking, "Is she going to be OK?" He replied, "I think so." I realized the question had to do with my response to what was coming next. My background as a farm girl was helpful. I knew what the insides of pigs and cows looked like, and, to my amazement, a person was not much different. The smell of the skull bone as the cap was removed by the saw was disconcerting, but the rest of the process was just interesting. Today, many TV shows include more blood and body details than I saw that day, but in the early 1980s, only medical students were privy to the inner workings of a human body. I felt privileged to have been present when the natural death of the prisoner was confirmed.

In Michigan prisons at that time, the two positions next in rank to the warden were the deputy and business manager. One controlled the bulk of the staff, the other controlled the money and supplies. In every prison where I have worked, there has been jockeying for power and position between those two employees. Paul Renico was an excellent business manager who rarely made mistakes. The deputy was good with security issues. Because the prison ran well, there was time left over for squabbling between the two. One memorable event involved painting the security fence. Paul had found a system that claimed to be good for spray painting. It involved running an electrical current through the fencing, which was supposed to cause the paint sprayed onto it to adhere. Even though the fence was on one side of the building and the parking lot on the other, gusts of wind off the lake carried droplets of paint to decorate staff vehicles. This was not discovered right away. Although some cars were washed promptly and the paint removed, we ended up hiring an outfit from Holland to come and wheel out the finish on several vehicles. The deputy managed to needle Paul about that for the rest of his time at the Dunes.

When we decided to build an Industries building and, later, an eighty-man housing unit, Paul and the deputy worked together to get those projects finished on budget without compromising security. One of the projects involved Amish builders. That was an opportunity to see religion's compromise with efficiency. The Amish workers were not permitted to interact directly with electricity; however, if someone else plugged in their saws and other electrically powered tools, they could use them. So, Dunes staff happily connected the cords so the Amish could work most productively.

To my dismay, the deputy continued to be an obstacle to my vision for the prison. When Denise Quarles, now the warden at Riverside in Ionia, asked me to help her interview a new deputy, I had an epiphany. Riverside was as close to my deputy's home as the Dunes, and he would get a one-level promotion if he became the deputy for Denise. She was being encouraged to hire a person with no custody experience and I was willing to hire and train that guy, so we cut a deal. She took my deputy and I hired Ray Tamminga as his replacement. That turned out to be a good deal for both of us. Sadly, I later lost Paul Renico when the Reformatory hired him as their business manager, but he had trained his assistant as a replacement, so I was happy to promote John Ingersoll.

As time passed and I mastered the routines of prison management, I started stretching the boundaries of the warden's role. One of the traditions in my mother's family was to bake cookies and make candy during the holidays to give as gifts to friends and teachers. When we moved to Michigan, my mother and we sisters continued that tradition. Because Christmas in prison is such a sad time, I decided to invite prisoners who did not get many visits to help me bake cookies in the food-tech training area and serve them to the prisoner population at a candlelight reception. I even suspended the rule that food could not be taken out of the dining room, and smiled at the sight of offenders with cookies stuffed into their shirts as they exited. A few staff joined me as bakers that first year and more came to help when we repeated the event.

While most staff seemed to be warming to my leadership style—which I described as Management by Wandering Around and Listening—one group still stymied me: the educators. A group of them were approaching as we walked the main corridor; I smiled and greeted them. I heard one say, after I had passed, "What do you think she meant by that?" That a smile with a simple "how're you doing?" would get such a response suggested trouble in paradise. As I talked with the school principal and his boss, the treatment director, I found that the teachers really did not feel like an integral part of the staff and that this had been the case since the prison opened. Also, I had initiated some changes in their area without consulting with them, which had increased their sense of alienation.

The budget had some room for hiring an expert to help heal this rift. Gordon Blush was a practicing psychologist with an interest in organizational dynamics. His spouse was in the education field, so he had some sense of education culture. We scheduled a three-day retreat at a local college where Dr. Blush led us through a series of assessments and exercises that gave us new ways to look at the conflicts we had experienced. I was especially enlightened by a classification tool which highlighted the characteristics of a leader who creates problems for line staff and of professionals who value stability and resist change. By offering staff a role in desired changes, and working through their concerns, changes can be owned by everyone involved. The leader still gets the needed result; it just takes patience and time. We all left the retreat with a better attitude toward our work together.

In fact, not long after the retreat, one of the teachers, Cassie Moore, suggested an activity that would mesh with her Job-Seeking Skills course. Since preparing a resume and practicing interviewing skills were included in her course, she thought it would offer prisoners a good experience if we invited local businesspeople to conduct the interviews. We had nearly four hundred volunteers coming to the facility, mostly for religious reasons, and it was not difficult to find some of those who would be willing to be interviewers. We were not sure prisoners would want to participate; as an incentive, we developed a sign-off card. If prisoners filled their card, to be signed after each interview, they would be entered in a drawing for a bucket of Kentucky Fried Chicken. That proved to be a motivator, and we had a lively evening of interviews. Both prisoners and interviewers pronounced the event a success. A few security staff raised the issue of chicken bones being potential weapons—a concern that did not materialize—so when we repeated the event the next year, we substituted pizza.

Another activity I initiated at the Dunes was Warden's Appreciation Day. That was an end-of-summer celebration dependent on having a "good" summer. We defined that as no disruptions on the yard or in the units. Since the riots at the major penitentiaries in May 1981, all prison staff worried about another round of prisoner uprisings. While the Prisoner Benefit Fund paid for the ice cream and hot dogs, staff were the servers, and that role reversal was much appreciated by the inmates. One year, we even had donkey softball—a variation on traditional softball where the participants, after a hit or walk, had to move to the next base with their assigned (live, miniature) donkey. Hilarity ensued when the uncooperative donkeys bucked, kicked, and broke loose. Some of the stronger prisoners even picked up their donkey and strode to their base. Who says there is no fun to be had in prison?

As an aside, Prisoner Benefit Fund revenues are derived from profits from the prisoner store. Each prison has a group of prisoners who determine, with staff assistance, how to use these funds. Typical expenses are cable TV, microwave ovens, refreshments and entertainment for holidays, and other items and activities not funded by the facility budget.

While I was settling into the warden's role, John was adjusting to a new high school. Fennville High proved to be a good fit for him. It was about the same size as Haslett and offered him a chance to play football and baseball, as well as receive decent academic preparation for college. When I moved to the Dunes, I asked Deputy Director Brown to leave me there until John finished high school. John had suffered through the long hours at Brighton and Jackson, the disruptions of a move, and two divorces. He deserved a period of stability when I could give him more time and attention. He earned his driver's license, got his first car, and was quite independent. We took turns making dinner; he handled his own laundry and helped around the house. When I started work on this book, John reminded me that I told him, in essence, that I needed him to take care of himself and give me no problems because I had been named the first woman to run a prison in Michigan and could not fail. His cooperation became an element essential to my success.

»»»»»»»»»»»

During the time I was at the Dunes, my father, Charles, had a heart attack and later, at Cleveland Clinic, a valve replacement. That experience converted him from a distant, difficult person to a loving father and grandfather who was not afraid to show affection. John wanted to save money for college, so he stayed with and worked for my parents at their rental store each summer. In his role as store owner, however, Charles sometimes reverted to his abusive ways. His favorite epithet directed at an employee who screwed up was, "You g—d—dummy." I recognized that from my youth. In a family that valued intelligence, that was the ultimate put-down. In contrast, my mother, Edna, had always offered unconditional love. Because John had spent so much time with them during his early years and was only five years younger than my youngest sister, he was treated like the son they had always wished for; unfortunately, verbal abuse was included along with an abundance of love.

»»»»»»»»»»»

Just before I began my time at the Dunes, Tekla Miller, one of my Network buddies, planned a cross-country ski party at her southeast Michigan home. All the other participants were couples and she said I could bring someone if I wanted. Since I was just out of a really bad marriage, I did not want to bring anyone who was relationship material. I remembered, though, that my old boss, Bill Kime, enjoyed cross-country skiing and thought I had heard that his wife was no longer in the picture. A phone call confirmed that and his willingness to join the party. He knew Luella Burke, who had worked for him, and knew of Tekla and Denise Quarles through their involvement in the Michigan Corrections Association. As the fates would have it, the weather did not cooperate with the skiing part of the party. We experienced one of Michigan's famous January thaws; a glorious, sunny day in the forties, which on Tekla's deck felt even warmer. I know that because I was very rude that day. Bill and I had a lot of catching up to do; we spent most of the party out on that deck, talking, laughing, and becoming a couple, even though neither of us had come to the gathering with that intention.

It was almost two hours from Bill's house in Dimondale to my apartment in Ganges. As an on-call warden, I had to be within an hour of the prison every other week. The deputy had that responsibility on the alternate week. So, as our relationship developed, Bill came to my place one weekend (occasionally bringing John's Haslett friend, Jim Christie) and I went to his the next. Sometimes, at midweek, we would have dinner in Grand Rapids. One of those meetings was a real test of the relationship. We had agreed to meet in the bar at a Brann's restaurant on Division Street. I arrived at the appointed hour, parked in the back, and went to the bar. So did Bill, although he parked on the street and came in the front entrance. After watching Bill check his watch with increasing frequency, the bartender asked him if he was waiting for someone. Bill said yes, but that I was often late. Then the bartender asked if Bill had checked the other bar in case I was waiting there—and I was! What were the odds that we would elect to meet at one of the few restaurants with two bars? Instead of being angry with each other, we laughed at the situation and enjoyed recounting that event.

»»»»»»»»»»»»

In August after I had arrived at the Dunes, I had a routine hysterectomy. I have always been sturdy and expected this to be an uneventful surgery. It was in most respects; however, there was a pesky low-grade infection that kept me at Holland Hospital several days longer than anticipated. Bill and I had planned for his children, Katie and Christopher, to come for a weekend at Lake Michigan to meet John and me. We did get to meet, but I was left in my hospital room while they went off to the lake. A complication of the infection was getting home after discharge without violating doctor's orders not to drive. My father was still recovering from surgery, so my mother was unavailable. John had not yet acquired his driver's license. Bill's schedule could not be revised. So, I drove myself home hoping not to get in an accident or rip any stitches. I again violated the initial doctor's orders by returning to work early. The doc and I were able to negotiate that I would remain outside the secure area of the prison and go home early on days when I became weary. I had good reason to return to work prior to the end of the six-week convalescence. My boss, the regional administrator, had decided to leave his office in Ionia and "help" by occupying my office and assuming administration of the Dunes. Regrettably, he did not enjoy the trust or respect of his wardens or their staff. I felt it was important to minimize his time at my prison.

»»»»»»»»»»»»

Before the surgery, I had arranged for a Michigan Corrections Association (MCA) conference at the Amway Grand Plaza Hotel in Grand Rapids. As the convention chair, I had to ensure we had a good program and enough people in attendance to cover expenses. Since the Department of Corrections used workshops at this conference as part of their professional training program, they helped with disseminating applications, but pricing and pulling together people to present a good program fell to me and the convention committee. Fortunately, I had been on the MCA board long enough to know who would deliver; we produced a great, well-attended conference in October.

As I mentioned earlier, my first taste of a national corrections conference left me wanting more. Bill and I attended three American Correctional Association conferences while I was at the Dunes, including those in Chicago and New York. At the former, both Bill and I were presenters, but we also managed to have dinner with Bob and Joy Brown and enjoy the ambiance of the Midland Hotel, where we were staying. To my delight, I found that there was a working group called the Women's Task Force within the American Correctional Association. Susan Hunter was active there and we renewed our friendship. Since I had met her, she had worked as a warden and was now with the National Institute of Corrections in Washington, DC. She introduced me to many other like-minded women, and we began to discuss how to raise the profile of women in the business. One downside of ACA: Luella and I were distressed to find scantily clad women at vendor booths in the exhibition hall and hectored the executive director about that. It took a few years, but staff for booths began to dress more professionally. At the state level, I was elected to the MCA board and encouraged the organization to provide one-day sessions around the state, so those who could not travel could still have the chance for training and to meet peers. I went to five of these in places as distant as Marquette and as close as Battle Creek, as well as two more of the annual three-day conferences.

Perry Johnson hosted the Association of State Correctional Administrators as he was ending his tenure as Michigan's director. He asked Luella Burke and me to arrange that gathering, and we found a great venue in West Michigan that resembled a castle. Warden Gary Wells and his wife Kay also hosted, opening their home in Spring Lake on the shore of Lake Michigan so that the participants could walk the beach and enjoy the view from their deck. Michigan State Industries made aprons with a stenciled image of the state as gifts for attendees as well as for those of us who volunteered to grill and serve the outdoor meal. Michigan offered beautiful June weather in 1984, and Perry pronounced it a grand ending to his time as director.

In addition to professional organizations, I wanted to nourish my relationships with women, so I found a chapter of the National Organization for Women in Saugatuck (Allegan County NOW) where I made friends with Lea Thrush and other locals. I also joined the Professional Women's Network based in Holland. With the former group, I attended the March for Women's Lives in Washington, DC, in March 1986, enduring a long bus ride for the thrill of filling the National Mall with passionate women from around the country demanding control of their bodies. The latter group was involved in my selection as the Holland Jaycee's Woman of the Year in 1984.

»»»»»»»»»»»

To my delight, Bill and I turned out to be good travel companions. We went to Toronto in 1983 before the May Wardens' Quarterly meeting. After a great visit, we drove to Traverse City, enjoying the varieties of pale greens of early spring. Our first test as travel mates was camping in the Canadian bush. Bill had gone on several major canoe camping expeditions with male friends that he called the Steel River trips. He wanted to share the beauty and solitude of those adventures with me. Of course, we did not have the time and I was not in shape for the entire trip he had made before. Consequently, he designed an abbreviated itinerary with only three portages that would end with a camp on Burnt Lake. We each carried a pack and, because Bill was a tall man, he had to carry the canoe most of the time. Only on level ground was I of any assistance with the canoe, and most of the trip was up and down hills. I survived with only sore muscles, but Bill stepped into a hole at the campsite; his ankle swelled up to twice the usual size. He soaked it in the cold lake without reducing the swelling but did get some relief from the pain. We managed to catch and cook tasty brook trout, avoid visits from bears, and thrilled to parades of loons with their babies as well as their haunting songs. When it was time to leave, I carried both packs out, making two trips to his one with the canoe. On the way home, we stopped at The Antlers in Sault Ste. Marie and could barely make it up and down the stairs. We were glad they served dirty, sweaty campers, because we were ready for someone else to cook for us. Like the "two bars" mishap at Brann's, what could have been a disaster became a story we enjoyed telling friends and family.

During my first two years at the Dunes, family ties provided ample opportunity to travel. Grandmother Withrow had moved to be near my paternal aunt, Barbara Ronksley, and her husband, Bob, in Pennsylvania. Sister Chere, her husband, Mike McCloskey, and sons, Mike Jr. and JP, lived in New Jersey. John and I combined visits to both states in one trip. He then flew to Florida to visit his father; I drove home with lobster for a late Fathers' Day celebration with Charles, Edna, and Kristy. The next year, my parents joined John and me for a Fathers' Day trip to New Jersey to meet Chere and Mike's newest addition, Matthew.

Sandwiched between the New Jersey trips was one to Corvallis, Oregon, with John, Chere, Kristy, Charles, and Edna for the wedding of my sister, Tina, to Brad Robinson. Tina was a feminist and hyphenated her name and convinced Brad to do so, too. So they became the Withrow-Robinsons. Tina and Brad had been drawn to the Friends meeting in Corvallis, so they were married Quaker-style, with no minister and a meditation period broken only when someone felt moved to speak. Because family had traveled from the East Coast and Midwest for the wedding, the newlyweds elected to spend their honeymoon with them in a rambling house on the Oregon coast.

It is unusual to have freezing weather and snow in Oregon. Nonetheless, Mother Nature decided to offer both for the wedding, creating two challenges. The first was transportation for the guests flying into Portland. I was dispatched for multiple trips because, as a Michigander, I knew how to drive in snow. True. However, the Oregonians on the road did not, and we were sharing the freeway. Happily, everyone arrived safely. Our second challenge was that the house at the coast suffered from freezing pipes. Again, happy to say, our family and the Robinson family got to know each other very well with no conflict. When the coast visit was over, John and I went on to San Francisco with Charles and Edna for a pleasant visit to that city. Poor Kristy had to go back to Michigan to help run the rental store while Chere returned to her family. It seemed like I had been gone a lot that first year at the Dunes because I had been. I was glad to return to the prison and continue to put my stamp on that facility.

»»»»»»»»»»»

Throughout the time at the Dunes, I enjoyed telling others about corrections. There are so many myths and misperceptions about prisons, and I found speaking to groups and classes a great way to offer my truth about the field I had chosen for a career. In December 1983, I was invited to be a speaker at Michigan State University's winter commencement. It was quite an experience to look over a huge auditorium filled with graduates and guests expecting words of wisdom; with that one under my belt, I felt like I could handle any other venue. My calendars for the Dunes reflect talks at the Quota Club in Grand Rapids, the Accountants Club in Zeeland, and the Kiwanis Club in Brighton. I also spoke to classes at Holland High School, Western Michigan University, Kellogg Community College, and Michigan State University. For the Department of Corrections, I served on panels in Bay City and Grand Rapids on the topic of public relations.

»»»»»»»»»»»»

As mentioned earlier, the prison was only a dune away from Lake Michigan. Not only did the Catholic Church give the state the seminary for a prison, but also woods and dunes of sufficient size to establish a state park. The park was still in the early stages of development and very lightly used when I arrived. There was no camping, and it was a long walk to the beach; although once you arrived, it was wonderful. The beach was sandy and the water shallow for a long way out, so it was great for families and those who wanted to go wading. I was a frequent visitor and loved the flowers, especially pink ladies' slippers in the spring. I also loved to walk among the fragrant pines all year long, and hike the dunes to get the long view of the lake.

Another part of the agreement with the local community was that there would be a state police post established in the mansion across from the prison. That beautiful home had served as a convent for a community of nuns. The state police needed only a small part of the space, and the lieutenant there was kind enough to let me ramble around the place. There was a ballroom on the top floor and, above that, a widow's walk that did permit a view of Lake Michigan. Dunes staff performed maintenance necessary to keep the heat, water, and lights functioning, but the structure needed serious work to bring it back to its glory days. At this writing, a community group in Saugatuck has undertaken the restoration of the Felt Mansion and offers it, and other buildings on the grounds, for event rentals.

Time went in a blink at the Dunes. In 1986, John graduated from high school and headed off to the University of Michigan. Robert Brown Jr. succeeded Perry in the director's job. About the time John graduated, Director Brown suggested that I interview for the warden's position at the Michigan Reformatory. It appeared that my idyllic stay in West Michigan was about to end. But not before some parties. First, I hosted a graduation open house for John at the Ganges apartment. Later, Dunes staff gave me a nice going-away party; Dutch wooden shoes painted with stripes were a memorable gift. It was sad to be leaving staff I had grown to love and a facility I knew well, but the challenge of running one of the state's old penitentiaries was one I could not pass up. The move would also put me an hour closer to Bill Kime, who had become not just a lover, but my best friend. As that relationship became more serious, John told me that if we ever tried to tie the knot, when the preacher got to the part where anyone with objections should speak, he would stand up and say that I was not very good at marriage. I had to acknowledge he was right; nevertheless, I felt Bill and I were headed in that direction.

»»»»»»»»»»»

Lesson Learned: When you have a problem staff person, sandwiching that person between you and another like-minded staffer helps neutralize their effects.

Corrections Story: A prisoner was being discharged from the Dunes. That meant the parole board did not want responsibility for that man in the community and, as a result, he had to serve the maximum term of his sentence. That prisoner was a charmer and managed to sell some of the religious volunteers a sad story about his lack of prospects upon release. Moved by Christian charity, the volunteers (without consulting staff) gave him a job as a night manager at a local grocery and provided him a furnished apartment. He rewarded their generosity by seducing the daughter of one of the volunteers and taking her to Las Vegas, intending to put her to work for him on the street. Fortunately, she managed a phone call to her parents, who rescued her. As a result, we augmented our volunteer orientation to include warnings about discharging prisoners and a requirement that volunteers' contact with former prisoners be reported to the prison.

7. THE REFORMATORY: EARLY YEARS

Blood on the floor every day. That was how my boss, Dan Bolden, described the Reformatory when I arrived. Even though we were five years post-riot, relations between staff and prisoners were abysmal. A year or so after the riot, John Jabe had replaced Dale Foltz, who moved to Jackson to restore order there. Warden Jabe's style was in stark contrast to his predecessor's. Foltz ran things through force of personality. Jabe wanted the prison to operate within policy guidelines. Staff had successfully stonewalled his efforts, predicting, accurately, that he would move on soon. And, sure enough, he was going to Jackson after three short years, to again take over from Foltz—who had retired. In July 1986, I became the first woman to run one of Michigan's three old penitentiaries. Even though many of the security staff reveled in the Reformatory's "Gladiator School" moniker, I was clear about the need to change their approach to prisoner management.

To begin, though, I needed a place to live and wanted it to be near the prison. Initially, that was a spartan motel room south of Ionia. I asked at the Chamber of Commerce if there were apartments available and Ruth Hewitt directed me to the home of Jack and Rosemary Westover. They had a small area upstairs that suited me exactly. It was across Wall Street from the Reformatory, in a house that had originally been built for a prison administrator. This was ideal for the short term, as it was now only fifty minutes from Ionia to Bill's home in Dimondale. Continuing to take the initiative, I asked him if we could get married. He thought about it and agreed that it would be a good idea. We wed on August 22, 1986, in the Westovers' living room. The prison chaplain was the officiant, with our children and the Westovers as witnesses. While my son did not carry out his threat to tell the minister why I should not be allowed to marry, Bill later told me that John had warned him I was not very good at matrimony.

Denise Quarles had by then tied the knot with another deputy director, Al Whitfield, and they hosted a reception for us at their home. Guests included Adria and Clay Libolt, Tekla Miller and her husband, Chet Peterson, and Luella and Arnold Burke. The Westovers agreed that Bill could visit on Wednesday nights. For the first year, I went to Dimondale on the weekends. While this was an inauspicious start for married life, I was working twelve- and fourteen-hour days and simply could not add a two-hour commute to that schedule. Bill was also working long hours trying to site and open a new prison every six weeks to handle the burgeoning prison population. Given our schedules, we were lucky to have any time together.

I knew it was going to be a challenge to run the oldest prison in the system. Early in my tenure, wanting to get a view of the physical plant and, remembering my days on Jackson's roof, I asked the shift commander if I could get to the top of the Rotunda, the high point of the prison. He detailed Lieutenant Doug Clark to escort me. After a five-story climb, Clark unlocked a gate and gestured to a wooden walkway that circled the base of the Rotunda roof. I wanted the best vantage point, so started climbing up the side of the roof. Before I reached the top, Clark said, "Ma'am, you are the warden and can go anywhere you want, but I think you should know that you are walking on glass." Why someone had decided to apply roofing shingles to a glass roof I do not know; however, I do know that I scrambled down with as much dignity as I could muster. Some years later, Clark confided that he could see his career ending if I crashed through the glass and ended up in a bloody heap in the middle of the Rotunda. Since he was a fine lieutenant, I was glad I heeded his warning.

As at the Dunes, I inherited a wonderful secretary. Barb Parks had been trained by an Ionia legend, Mary Esther Daddazio, who demanded perfection from her workers. Barb was quietly efficient and, while never questioning my actions, she could raise an eyebrow in a way that told me I was on the wrong track. When I tried to send out an internal communication with an inked correction, she patiently retyped it, explaining that the warden's office should always set the standard for the prison. The deputy had interviewed for the warden's job. Fortunately, Jabe decided to take him along to Jackson, so I did not have another disappointed deputy situation. Marsha Foresman was my administrative assistant, and I was sorry that Jabe also stole her. She was familiar with the consent decree—more about that later—and I thought we would have worked well together; however, she was offered a promotion that I could not match.

As for the other staff, not all were delighted that I was to be their leader. Many of them were quite open about their distaste for a woman boss. In fact, one inspector retired, saying he would not work for any g—d— woman. I heard about his comment, went to his retirement party, and wished him well. The party was in Hubbardston, a particularly insular and conservative area of Ionia County, and I can admit today that I feared that I would be run off the road or physically attacked by a staff member whose inhibitions had been lowered by alcohol. Fortunately, I just got hard looks and a frosty reception. On one hand, I was sorry to see that inspector leave, because he was experienced and had a good reputation as a security specialist; on the other hand, he was said to encourage physical retaliation for prisoner misconduct, an action I was determined to end.

The prisoners housed inside were challenging, primarily due to their age. These young men were ages eighteen to twenty-one, plus a few juveniles as young as fifteen, who had been waived to adult prison due to the seriousness of their crime. Without experience in an adult prison, they were constantly testing the limits; in addition, their youth meant their impulse control was limited. Also, those with life or long sentences went through something akin to what a dying person faces. First, they were in denial, then angry, then they began bargaining, which in prison meant appealing their sentence. Eventually, most worked their way to acceptance, but that was sometimes after they had transferred from the Reformatory.

When the age limit was raised to twenty-six, we all breathed a sigh of relief. Some of the older prisoners had experience doing time and helped school the youngsters in proper prison conduct. That sometimes also brought schemes and scams we did not appreciate, but, overall, the expansion of the age range was a benefit. At the minimum-security dorm, the youthfulness of the offenders did not create the same problems. In part, I think this was because the prisoners knew they had little time to do and that acting out would lead to a bed in higher security and possibly a delay in parole. Also, the nature of the crimes for which dorm prisoners were serving were usually less serious, and especially, less violent.

Then there was the physical plant. The original prison was built in 1877 and had a central rotunda with four two-story wings. When I arrived only one wing still housed prisoners—those segregated as management problems. This unit was called the Adjustment Center. Offenders needing protection were on higher floors of one of the "new" blocks added in the late 1930s. There was an industrial laundry, a combined furniture factory and maintenance building, a cannery that had been converted to vocational education, and a chow hall with an auditorium above it. Health Care was in a wing off the Rotunda, as were offices for the deputy and his staff. Quartermaster and Hobbycraft were in other wings; some wings were unused. The newest building was a chapel, built with donated funds and located next to the fenced recreation yard. The school had been burned in the riot and replaced by modular units. An armed post overlooked the yard; there were other posts strategically placed around the walls. The visiting room was between pedestrian sally port gates.

Across Wall Street was the minimum-security dorm from which workers came to handle grounds care, maintenance, the warehouse, the power plant, and cleaning chores outside the secure perimeter. The dorm had a school, and recreation and visiting rooms, but no fences. A house at the corner of Main and Wall had been converted to provide the trainer's office and training space for prison employees. Administrative offices and the arsenal were in an addition in front of the original construction.

As at Jackson, there was a shoeshine stand in the Rotunda. The prisoner assigned to this job was in a prime position to overhear staff conversations and thus, to my mind, posed a security risk. There was a mezzanine area on the second level of the Rotunda. To my dismay, the Jaycees and the prison newspaper staff were in makeshift offices on that mezzanine. Just like the shoeshine worker, these prisoners had a prime location for gathering intelligence about staff and operations. I had always disliked the tradition of a shoeshine stand in a prison and was glad I could offer a security reason for ending that assignment. Even though shift supervisors acknowledged the potential for prisoners gathering personal and prison information in that job, elimination of the stand was not a popular move. The fact that the prisoners objected mightily to the relocation of their "offices" to less sensitive areas confirmed my belief that the initial sites were not in the facility's best interests. As an aside, I will note that prisoners' knowledge of a staff member's divorce or financial distress can put that staff member in a vulnerable position, potentially subject to pressure to smuggle items into the prison or assist in an escape.

After making these unpopular changes, the next challenge was to get staff to understand that I was here for the duration and that they needed to follow my lead or find a new home. The latter option was available, because the DOC was opening new prisons rapidly throughout the state, many within driving distance of Ionia. I was dismayed that staff seemed to revel in their physical confrontations with prisoners. It was the practice, I was told, if a prisoner assaulted staff, to drag the assailant down the concrete stairs by their heels, with their heads bouncing off the steel facing of each step. Then, the handcuffed offender would be bounced off the walls of a long corridor and dragged across the Rotunda to the Adjustment Center. Since I did not believe violence by staff would engender good behavior by prisoners, I made a point of discouraging use of force and disciplining staff who violated that policy.

A prime opportunity was presented the day a prisoner knocked an officer to the floor in the chow hall. Other staff responded promptly and subdued the prisoner, face-down, across a table. The assaulted officer jumped up and slammed a closed fist into the prisoner's face. Not only did other prisoners report the officer's conduct, but staff confirmed it. I fired the officer. In Michigan, corrections officers have a strong union in addition to civil-service protections, so he was eventually returned to work and the prison ordered to give him back pay for the time he was off. However, as I have mentioned, prisons are like small towns and, in this case, the grapevine whispered that the officer owed significant child support. Social Services somehow got wind of the officer's impending windfall and diverted it to support his children. I thought justice prevailed in that instance.

As I was encouraging staff to follow policy, I discovered that policy and procedure manuals were not available to staff in housing units or on posts and could find no evidence that staff were given this information by any other method. The department had entered into a federal consent decree, which meant outside experts were visiting regularly and scrutinizing operations, so I directed that supervisors develop systems for communicating policy and updating staff on procedural changes. In addition, as at Jackson and the Dunes, I spent a lot of time walking and talking with both staff and prisoners while observing daily operations.

Employees of Prison Industries and Health Care did not report to me, but I was responsible for security in their areas, so visited frequently and got to know the workers. During that first year, a prisoner working in the furniture factory was missed at count. We reviewed possibilities for his escape. Over the wall during the day seemed unlikely. Vehicles leaving the facility had been properly searched, so we did not think he had left that way. As a result, I reported the prisoner missing, but refused to say he had escaped. By the second day, Director Brown was losing patience. We had brought in a state-police dog to search the factory with no success. Brown strongly urged me to declare the prisoner an escapee. I defended the staff and said I was sure he was still inside. We had prisoner informants who had told us food was being smuggled into the furniture factory, and we believed it was for that missing prisoner. Sure enough, around 5:00 a.m. on the third day, I was awakened by the sound of a shotgun blast. The prisoner had topped the wall next to the furniture factory. The post officer shouted at him to stop. When he jumped outside the wall instead, the officer fired a warning shot. Since the prisoner had broken both ankles during his landing, he was not going anywhere. Staff secured him and brought him to the Rotunda to await transport for medical attention. I spoke with him before he left and found that he had been hiding in a sawdust bin most of the time, which was why the state-police dog had not scented him. As a sad aside, when I called his mother to inform her that he was safe—but with ankles broken—she disclosed that she was an orthopedic nurse and knew those breaks would plague him the rest of his life.

As a result of this incident, my relations with staff improved. They knew I had defended their actions and refused to say the prisoner had managed to defeat our security systems. Bill Kime, however, reminded me that sometimes one was just lucky, not good. I preferred to think that the luck was created by all the walking, listening, and observing I had been doing. While people outside the prison might find it hard to understand how someone could hide inside for nearly three days, I knew about the many nooks and crannies in that old place and had no problem believing it.

»»»»»»»»»»»»

My bosses continued to find training opportunities for me and for others who were experiencing rapid promotions. One was at the Wharton School in Philadelphia. One session in that leadership seminar was quite memorable. Participants were divided into four groups by gender and ethnicity—white men, white women, minority men, and minority women. Each group was asked to consider four questions. What was it like to be a member of their own group working in corrections and what was it like to be a member of each of the other three? Each group would then report to the others the result of their discussions. We all went into private spaces and three of the four groups followed the directions. Unfortunately for them, the white males got so caught up in discussing what it was like to be white men working in corrections that they ran out of time to consider the ramifications for others. They decided to report that it was about the same for everyone else. Since the other groups had reported that they perceived significant differences for the various groups, the white males' report was not well received. The white men received quite direct feedback. Their approach to this task, they were told, reflected their lack of sensitivity about what it was like to be a minority of any type in the corrections business. The other groups were unanimous in their perception that the role of the minority female was hardest. White women thought it was harder for them than for minority men, and minority men thought just the opposite. A white man from Michigan later told me that he tried to get his group on task because he knew what would happen when we reconvened, but had no success. I do think some of the white guys got a wake-up call about gender and racial differences in the workplace.

At the end of that session, I was asked to co-facilitate a similar session with a Wharton trainer the following summer in Denver. Always up for a challenge, I agreed to do so. The session went well, and I celebrated by staying at a nice bed and breakfast in downtown Denver. It had a good French restaurant where

I had an excellent dinner. After dinner, I decided to go for a stroll in my red silk dress with a little black bag hanging from my shoulder. The block from the B & B to the main street was not well lit, but I could see lots of pedestrian traffic at the end of the block. I lit a cigar and took off. I passed a young man who appeared to be sleeping near the sidewalk. He was not asleep; he leaped up and tugged the bag from my shoulder. The chain broke and the bag fell to the ground. When he bent to retrieve it, I beat him on the back with my lit cigar, yelling that he had no business stealing my bag. I recall seeing the sparks on his white shirt and hoping he would have to explain burn holes to his mom. He ran off down an alley and I stood at the end and shouted at him to take the money but leave the ID because I had a plane to catch. My plea was accepted, and the bag tossed toward me. By then, the commotion had attracted onlookers, who expressed concern and offered assistance. I asked them to watch me get the bag in case the assailant returned. By the time I got back to the B & B, the foolishness of my response had registered. What if the guy had pulled a knife or a gun? I certainly was not prepared to deal with that. I had left most of my cash and all of my credit cards in the room, so the robber got $40. I must have looked a little wobbly when I got back to my lodging because the proprietors gave me a glass of brandy and were very solicitous. I declined to call the police. This was not a serious crime; I just wanted to curl up in my room and be thankful I was not harmed.

»»»»»»»»»»»»

In 1987, Lansing Community College asked that I join their corrections advisory board. Since that school had been instrumental in helping me find funds for my own education, I was happy to say yes. I taught for Montcalm Community College and, in 1988, they also requested I join their advisory board. In both cases, the meetings were quarterly and offered the opportunity for input for the classes the colleges provided students. All corrections officers were required by law to have eighteen semester or twenty-three term credits before they could be hired; most students acquired these credits at community colleges. It made sense to have what they learned in their classes meet the needs of the prisons.

»»»»»»»»»»»»

When Bill retired in 1988, we found a home in Ionia. Only fifteen minutes from the prison, it was at the end of a long gravel drive on a wooded ridge within walking distance of the Grand River. We spent hours visiting the adjacent woods and fields, identifying wildflowers, and getting to know our new neighborhood. The people from whom we bought the home kept some acreage and built next door. They operated Wilson's Heating and Cooling and we enjoyed getting to know Bill, Nancy, and their children Cara, Billy, and Lauren. Also living on that ridge were Bob and Maria Martinez, who were wonderful neighbors. Those who hunted used the woods for the fifteen days of firearm deer season; the rest of the time, it was ours to explore.

In retirement, Bill learned to cook and usually had dinner ready when I came home from the prison. In addition, he took on cleaning duties, although he called his standards "goat gagging." (If it would not gag a goat, it was clean enough.) He enjoyed planning vacations and sometimes took pre-vacation trips to scout locations. His children had settled in San Diego and Houston, and trips often included visits with them, or to see Tina and Brad in Oregon. By the time we moved to Ionia, I was only working ten-hour days and bringing a briefcase of paperwork home. After dinner, I would clean up, we would chat, and then it was back to prison business for me. At least I was able to be home with Bill. He usually read while I worked and did not complain about being ignored.

Despite the long hours, I became involved with local service organizations. Mary Esther Daddazio recruited me for the Business and Professional Women's Group in 1986. I was invited to speak at the Rotary club, and one member mentioned that the wardens were usually members. Rotary International had just opened their membership to women and, to my delight, Denise Quarles, then the warden at Riverside, and I were brought into Rotary at the same time. My father had been an active Rotarian in Okemos and was proud to come to my induction and present my official Rotary badge. The club lost a few members over the inclusion of their first female members, but most welcomed us, and some became good friends.

The Chamber of Commerce had an ambassador group that I joined to be part of ribbon-cutting events and help with parades. When I found that the domestic violence shelter needed volunteers, I asked to work with the children housed there. We read stories, painted, colored, and created seasonal crafts. Sadly, that pleasure ended when some of the women housed there expressed concern that their children might mention that their daddy worked at the prison I ran. Thus, I was transitioned to the advisory board. While that was not as much fun as working with the kids, I did meet Maureen Burns, Mary Foy, and Pat Hinrichs. Their friendship yielded fun dinners, good conversation, and support at critical times. Because the department was expanding so rapidly, new corrections officers were being hired as fast as they could be found. Montcalm Community College had a satellite site at the high school in Ionia, and I taught two corrections officer classes there during the year I lived with the Westovers.

The first winter at the Reformatory, Bill and I went to Sault Ste. Marie over Presidents' Day weekend to cross-country ski with Bob and Lynn LeCureux and other corrections friends. Bob was the warden at Kinross and shared my values about prison operations. Bill liked Bob because he loved the outdoors and was another fisherman, and especially because he enjoyed Bill's jokes and awful puns. For several years, that weekend was reserved for a trip north. Luella and Arnold Burke often came, as did Denise Quarles and Al Whitfield. Whitefish dinner at the Ojibway Hotel spiced with good conversation was a highlight. The skiing was enjoyed more by some than others, but everyone usually participated for at least part of the trip—until injury, exhaustion, or cold forced us indoors. February in the Upper Peninsula can be brutal. One morning, our departure was delayed because it was so cold that nobody could get a vehicle started. That became one more story to tell the next time we gathered.

Bill often said either Lecureux or I would have been wonderful directors, but were too smart to want that job. I am not sure it was due to intelligence. In Bob's case, it was because of his love for Michigan's Upper Peninsula and the outdoor recreation it offered. He and Lynn had a beautiful home on the St. Mary's River and many family members and friends to keep them happy there. For me, the lack of a poker face was a handicap. When angry or upset, the color begins to rise on my neck. Paul Renico once remarked to those in a meeting, "You might as well quit arguing with her when the red gets to her earlobes. She won't hear anything you say after that." I can testify that he was speaking from experience. In addition, I loved the immediate rush of daily prison operations and hated meetings. At the Reformatory, the standard was that we would meet for one hour. If it was clear we could not get to closure, the meeting was adjourned to gather information needed for resolution, and a future time and place identified when we would try again. Staff learned to be prepared and succinct. Best of all, we did not waste precious time.

Wardens as a group, however, were forced to attend quarterly meetings. These were to impart information and lasted three days. We met all over the state, but often gathered near Traverse City or Lansing. The former because it was centrally located for both Upper and Lower Peninsula staff and the latter because it was convenient for those coming from Central Office. While I was at the Dunes, I enjoyed these meetings. They were a mini vacation at state expense. Bill was usually in attendance and that gave me more time with him, a plus from my point of view. Also, there were under a dozen institution heads. However, once I had the responsibility of the Reformatory, I resented the time away. The information we were given was purely one-way. Various officials from Central Office would lecture us about their areas of expertise, we would hear about the impact of budget and prisoner population, new wardens would be introduced, and I would knit and worry about what was going on back at the joint. That intimate group of wardens I had liked had grown and would continue to grow dramatically, diminishing the camaraderie I had so much enjoyed. The major benefit of the expansion was the addition of other women wardens. Luella, Denise, and Tekla became my peers and made those meetings much more enjoyable. Pat Caruso, who later became the agency's first female director, was also welcomed into our sisterhood.

I will mention at this point that, when I started at the Dunes, not all prison heads were called wardens. That term was reserved for those who ran Jackson, Marquette, and the Reformatory. The rest were called superintendents, had smaller operations, and were paid slightly less. When I moved to the Reformatory, I got a pay raise and much more responsibility. As a wave of new prisons opened in the 1990s, the distinction was harder to maintain, and, eventually, the DOC decided to call everyone who ran a prison a warden.

At the end of the first summer at the Reformatory, I decided to have a Warden's Appreciation Day, and brought in donkey softball. This silly activity was a way to let staff know we were going to have some fun while running a safe and secure prison. It was also intended to advise prisoners that relations with staff were going to improve. While the event was not an unqualified success, things went smoothly and, at the end of the second summer, we tried it again. This time we brought in a vendor to distribute hot dogs from a carnival-style cart. Unfortunately, a prisoner with a beef to settle brought a prison-made truncheon to the yard and assaulted a fellow inmate. Blood was all over, including on the vendor's cart. We got him safely out of the area, and, when he was later interviewed by staff to see if he was traumatized by the experience, he grinned and said he was not. In fact, he claimed he would make extra money on his fair circuit telling about his experiences at the Reformatory.

That ended warden appreciation activities. However, for holidays, the Prisoner Benefit Fund would sometimes come up with ideas for special food or entertainment. One Fourth of July, they hired a singer called Mona Sally. Her act was staged in the vehicle sally port next to the yard. When she started singing and strutting her stuff in a skintight catsuit, she caused a near riot. Prisoners certainly got their money's worth that year. The recreation director who had engaged Miss Mona was strongly encouraged to find less provocative entertainment in the future.

»»»»»»»»»»»»

Much of my time in those early years was spent ensuring we met the provisions of the federal consent decree that resulted from the 1981 riots. I understood why the agency had entered into the decree instead of pursuing litigation with the Department of Justice. Many of the physical plant changes needed would not have been funded without federal oversight. It made more sense to allocate scarce state funds for needed improvements instead of for litigation costs. The agreement was divided into broad areas, including fire safety, sanitation, overcrowding and protection from harm, classification, physical health, and mental health. There may have been others, but those were the ones I recall having the most impact. Fire safety required the construction of smoke compartments and fire escapes. Sanitation required the replumbing of the cell blocks to prevent cross-contamination and permitted upgrades in food service equipment. Out-of-cell time became an issue related to overcrowding and protection from harm and let us remodel the seldom-used auditorium into a gymnasium that was extremely popular with the prisoners. Fortunately, technology allowed us to monitor and record in the area, which kept the violence to a minimum. While physical and mental health providers were not my responsibility, ensuring on-time arrival of prisoners with appointments for those services was. Staff balked at the recordkeeping that was required to document compliance; however, we were visited regularly by the court's expert witnesses and recordkeeping soon became routine. Judge Enslen was strict about compliance with the decree and occasionally warned department employees to "bring a toothbrush" if they came to court without complying with one of his orders. I do not think anyone ever actually went to jail for contempt, but Enslen certainly had our attention. On one of the few occasions I had to attend a hearing, I brought my knitting. The bailiff advised me that I could not knit in court as it distracted the judge.

From a security standpoint, the riskiest construction project was the installation of an elevator. This was needed to deliver food to the five levels of segregation on the outside of I-Block. A hole in the wall had to be cut on each floor to access the elevator. Additionally, a new exercise area outside the wall was constructed for segregation and protection prisoners. This required an electronic perimeter monitoring system. Not trusting the system, the shift commander usually also had an armed officer stationed near that yard whenever prisoners were there.

Another area requiring attention was maintenance. In the 1970s, when the department's population was declining, the Reformatory had been targeted for closure by 1990 and most routine maintenance activities had been deferred. Roofs, especially, needed attention, as did painting and repairs throughout. When the population soared with changes in the calculation of prisoner time off for good behavior and the end of automatic time cuts designed to keep prison counts manageable, the closure plan was abandoned. In addition to consent decree projects, the maintenance department had more work orders than they had time or funding to handle. I recall brainstorming how to fit some of the more pressing needs under the consent decree umbrella, as that always had priority as well as a funding stream separate from the Reformatory's budget.

Even though attention to the facility's operation was a priority, attention to professional development and personal survival were also important. To meet those needs, I attended most summer and winter conferences of the American Correctional Association (ACA), where I was a presenter at a session entitled "What is a Warden?" and served on the Long-Term Institutions Committee and the Women's Task Force. That group was chaired by Susan Hunter and I was delighted to have an opportunity to rekindle a relationship with her. Because corrections was opening to women nationwide and members of the task force were often future leaders, we decided to host a reception at the summer conference and encourage commissioners and directors to attend and meet women from throughout the country. I offered to arrange the reception and seek sponsors for the first one, and, with the help of others, continued to do that for several years. Susan's role in the National Institute of Corrections made her a natural facilitator between agency heads and job seekers. She continued her advocacy for diversity in the field and set a wonderful example for us all.

In conjunction with ACA were meetings of the North American Association of Wardens and Superintendents (NAAWS). At the NAAWS meetings, I learned that wardens around the country were sharing my struggles and gained insights from those with more experience and knowledge. Happily, I rekindled a friendship with Sharon Johnson Rion at these meetings, also. In fact, it was at a NAAWS meeting that my relationship with Sharon was cemented. She had worked her way through the NAAWS offices and was slated to be elected president for the 1991-92 term. She would be the first woman to head the organization; perhaps a more controversial element was that it would also be the first time anyone from the private prison sphere would helm NAAWS. Motivated by one or both factors, an old-guard group put together an alternate slate of candidates which changed only one position. Sharon was replaced by someone they deemed more suitable. When she discovered this, she came to me both angry and upset—to the point of throwing in the towel. After some discussion, she decided to fight instead. She knew many NAAWS members, primarily women and minorities, who did not ordinarily attend NAAWS meetings. She and I contacted all those we could locate and urged that they attend the meeting. Imagine the shock of the old-guard group when they came to the meeting and saw a room full of people they did not know belonged to NAAWS. Better yet, when they presented their alternate slate, the person they nominated for president shocked them. He stood up and declared that Sharon had worked hard for the organization and earned her shot at the presidency and that he respectfully declined the nomination. Someone then moved the original slate be adopted and Sharon prevailed.

This marked a turning point for the organization. Those who had rallied to help elect her stayed involved to create a more dynamic group focused on leadership training. In addition to the meetings associated with ACA, leadership conferences were held annually. Plans for a book, to be published by ACA, were initiated under Sharon's watch. To ensure it came to fruition, she served as the first editor. It is titled *A View from the Trenches* and contains monographs authored by people who have actually been responsible for running jails and prisons. The first edition was published in 1999, and Sharon designed it as a binder to allow readers to add content they thought relevant. In 2007, I edited the second edition; serendipity allowed it to be published the year Luella Burke was NAAWS president. A third edition is on the way as I write this.

Another conference I enjoyed was Women Working in Corrections and Juvenile Justice (WWICJJ). While ACA and NAAWS had formal structures, WWICJJ was an outgrowth of ACA's Women's Task Force and a grassroots effort that somehow managed to produce a national conference every two years. I attended my first WWICJJ conference in Portland, Oregon, in 1989 and enjoyed the energy and enthusiasm that the women exhibited.

»»»»»»»»»»»»

The ACA presentation I mentioned came about because I had been tapped to assist the National Institute of Corrections in developing a competency profile for wardens and superintendents. I suspect my friend Susan Hunter had a hand in selecting me for that task. Seven wardens met in Boulder, Colorado, in the fall of 1988 to brainstorm the various duties involved in managing prisons. In the end, we identified twelve areas and 142 tasks associated with running a prison. In no particular order, these involved managing people, the external environment, litigation, change, the office, inmates, security processes, emergencies, and the budget. Also included were reviewing and inspecting operations and the physical plant, maintaining professional competence and awareness, and developing long- and short-term goals and objectives. The discussions that produced these elements were important to me because I was struggling to change the Reformatory's culture. Time away from the prison with like-minded wardens gave me new resolve to tackle the work and better tools with which to approach it.

»»»»»»»»»»»»

Probably the hardest part of the early years at the Reformatory was my relationship with the deputy. I was fortunate to have inherited Paul Renico as business manager. He had been at the facility long enough to have a handle on operations and was seasoned in his role. However, hiring a deputy was a major opportunity to let staff know we were headed in a new direction. After conducting interviews, the best candidate was a Black woman. Uncertain whether those in Central Office would support the selection, I scheduled an appointment with Director Brown. He knew the woman, of course, and knew she was likely to be difficult to manage; however, he did not share my concern about the prison being headed by two females. He pointed out that prisons had been run by two men for years and he did not see how having the Reformatory headed by two women should be any different. Clearly, he was further along the path to embracing diversity than I was. I hired the best candidate, and she was difficult. She was also a great role model and tough manager. Staff tried to create divisions and I sometimes had to make rounds in her company to dispel rumors that we were at odds. When she was promoted, I was sorry to see her go.

By the end of the first five years at the Reformatory, there was no longer blood on the floor every day. I had not heard "Gladiator School" as our nickname in a while. Consent decree construction was well under way with some projects completed. The number of management segregation cells had been increased and the need for protection beds had decreased. When it was suggested that we attempt to become accredited through the American Correctional Association in a limited number of areas, I was offended. While our prison was old, accreditation standards were primarily about operations, not physical plant. Not one mandatory standard was impossible to meet due to the facility's construction. As a result, I asked that we attempt full accreditation. That request was granted, although some were skeptical about our chance to achieve it, and we began our next round of adventures.

»»»»»»»»»»»»

Lesson Learned: State the nonnegotiables at every opportunity. Violence against prisoners is unacceptable. A clean, orderly prison is a way of demonstrating control. Giving respect is a way of getting respect. Listen.

Corrections Story: The Ionia Free Fair used prisoner workers from the dorm during the spring and summer. These workers were supervised by Free Fair staff with Reformatory supervisors stopping by occasionally to confirm that all was well. During a slow time, civilian workers decided to use the prisoners to wash their personal cars, giving them cash for that service and even letting them move the cars. The temptation was too much for one prisoner. With cash in hand, he took off in one of the cars, bought liquor at a local store, and returned to work. His absence was unnoticed! We found out about these events when he returned to the dormitory, drunk, and disclosed the events of his happy day.

8. THE REFORMATORY: MIDDLE YEARS

There were so many events and initiatives during the second five years at the Reformatory that it is hard to know where to begin. I got a second chance at hiring a deputy. Due to staff reductions in Michigan State Industries, one of their employees was to be bumped into the deputy's vacancy. He had no security experience and really did not want the job, but civil-service rules would have sent him into it anyway. On the other hand, the Reformatory's business manager, Paul Renico, aspired to be a warden and saw the deputy's slot as a stepping-stone to that goal. It took some work with Human Resources to make it happen, but Gary Pierson was finally installed as the business manager and Paul as deputy. Both were well-suited for their positions and a period of stability and relative tranquility ensued.

»»»»»»»»»»

On a sad personal note, in the fall of 1992, my father finally succumbed to complications from a heart-valve replacement. One bright side of his long illness was that he had become a loving father and grandfather. His and my mother's concerns about the dangerousness of my work at the Reformatory had been reduced by a visit during count time one late afternoon. The prisoners were locked up, but my parents were able to see that the place was much more humane than the grim walls and towers made it seem. They had sold the family rental business and were looking forward to a long retirement together; however, that was not to be. My mother was distracted from her grief by Kristy's need for help with her son, Salem, while Kristy attended Ferris State University in pursuit of a pharmacy degree. Not long after Charles passed, Chere and Mike moved back to Michigan, so Edna had three of her girls close by for support.

»»»»»»»»»»»

Some one-time activities took place during this period. In 1992, dorm prisoners assisted the city of Ionia and community volunteers in creating a series of wooden play structures at a park in Ionia. The offenders set huge poles during the rainy first day and returned to the dorm muddy and worn out but satisfied with their contribution to the effort. They worked alongside Ionia citizens for the next two days. Later, at the dedication, they earned a big round of applause when they sang "Jailhouse Rock."

Many high schools in the area wanted presentations about prisons and prisoners; I had fun developing a presentation that was interactive. I sewed together a couple of sheets to make a base the size of a cube in a temporary facility. This was the sleeping area for six prisoners and, in addition to three bunk beds, contained three desks, three chairs, and six wall lockers. Prisoners could also have a personal footlocker, which was to be stored under the bunk. Strips of fabric were applied to indicate the spaces occupied by the furnishings. Prisoners accompanied me on these speaking engagements. I would describe a typical day and then invite six high-school volunteers to come and act out the process of getting up, dressed, and out the door for the breakfast meal. The prisoners would then critique the students' acting. One thing the students did not consider was that theft was likely if all the prisoners were absent from the cube. It had no door. The lockers were cheaply made, and the backs could be pried off easily. According to the prisoners, one man had to remain in the cube at all times to guard against theft. Meals would be smuggled out of the chow hall for the guy left behind. I suspect the officers turned a blind eye to this because they were unable to provide adequate security. If someone got ripped off, a confrontation could occur, and prevention made the most sense. After the students were done with their role playing, they were invited to question the prisoners, with the understanding that the offenders did not have to answer questions they considered out of line. These presentations continued until the officers' union decided that I should not be able to escort prisoners without a custody officer present. There were no funds to pay for an officer to go along for such purposes, so that form of presentation ended.

In 1993, Calvin College developed a choir comprised of their students and Reformatory prisoners. That continued for a second year. Calvin also provided an educational opportunity called "Interim" with accelerated hands-on learning. Jacki Lyden with National Public Radio recorded a program on juvenile lifers in which some prisoners and I were featured.

When 1993 ended, we had experienced only one dorm escape. Given that we had thirty-three prisoners leave without permission the year before I arrived, this was significant. One element supporting the historical escapes was a natural route over the Grand River via an unused railroad bridge. Prisoners would then go through the small town of Saranac and make their way to the freeway, where an arranged pickup would occur. Or a vehicle theft would offer an exit. One memorable escape ended in a Los Angeles suburb when two escapees were captured after a high-speed chase. They had stolen a pickup truck in Saranac. The driver had thoughtfully left his keys and wallet on the floor of the vehicle. Using his credit cards to buy gas, the escapees had made it all the way to the West Coast. Ironically, the police were unaware they were about to apprehend prison escapees from Michigan; they initiated the traffic stop because the tailgate of the truck had been left down.

A single fence topped with razor wire had been erected around the dorm, which discouraged escapes; however, another attempted escape ended when one of the participants was badly cut by the razor wire. Rather than leave his injured partner, the second would-be escapee returned with him to the dorm for medical treatment. Not all prisoners are bad guys, after all.

»»»»»»»»»»»»

Another first-woman honor came my way in 1993. A local financial institution, Independent Bank, decided that it was time to add a woman to their board. I had been in Rotary with the bank's president and he apparently thought I would be a good fit. As a result, I got to find out how community banks work. The monthly meetings were in the morning, so I would take annual leave or adjust my schedule. I do not recall any occasion when my work for the department created a conflict of interest, although I did have to report the employment every year. I decided to take payment in stock, rather than be paid directly. That turned out to be a bad choice. During the 2008 fiscal crisis, the bank made a ten-for-one reverse stock split, and the value of my shares shrunk precipitously. By then, I had retired from the board, so I could not even grouse to management. Since I was not depending on these stocks to finance my retirement, no serious harm was done.

»»»»»»»»»»»»

In 1994, a gospel rock band, DC Talk, made a music video called "The Hard Way" at the facility, which featured prisoners. The video can be viewed on YouTube today. NBC Nightly News with Brian Williams and Entertainment

Tonight also visited inside the prison that year. As part of a Prison Fellowship fundraiser, columnist Cal Thomas came to the facility, along with 210 citizens who joined prisoners for a meal in the inmate dining room. People who had never had contact with prisoners or prisons had a chance to learn about their tax dollars at work that night. All of these were potentially risky events; however, staff and prisoners were up to the task. Michigan corrections got some good publicity and I felt we were beginning a cultural shift.

During this time, computers were introduced to the Reformatory. The first challenge was to convince Barb Parks to give up her beloved typewriter. Since she was aware that she set the standard for support staff, she reluctantly learned to use this new tool. I am not sure she ever learned to love the computer, but she made the conversion with little complaint. A bigger challenge was the control center. This space housed three shifts, and the regular sergeant for each shift was the person most affected. Recalling the lessons from the Dunes and school staff there, I left the details to the three shifts, stating only that we needed to begin to use this new tool and that there were funds for remodeling the control center, but that all three shifts needed to agree on the design and placement of computers. Sgt. Pat Kelley was probably the most resistant. I think he was finally persuaded when I equated the computer with other tools we used in the business. We had introduced new rifles and staff did not necessarily embrace them, but those were the tools we needed to use, so we learned to qualify with them. The computers were replacing typewriters and we needed to learn how to use these new tools, also. While he was initially reluctant, I think that Sgt. Kelley would have objected mightily if I had tried to take away his computer after the first year. And staff did collaborate and develop a functional control center.

The initiative of most immediate consequence was the work leading to accreditation. While the American Correctional Association boasted that no accredited prison had ever been successfully sued over conditions of confinement, that did not excite staff because we were already in the middle of a federal consent decree that included conditions of confinement issues and more. To motivate them, I shamelessly goaded staff with the truth that my bosses were skeptical of our ability to achieve accreditation. It was true that policy compliance was not the Reformatory's strong suit; however, policies often were based on ACA standards and accreditation was a vehicle to move us in that direction.

In preparation for the auditors' visit, all supervisors were tasked with visiting areas under their supervision and ensuring that these were compliant with ACA standards. In my case, that meant the whole place, and, even though I was inside the facility more than most wardens and thought I had been in all areas during the first five years, I still discovered a space in one of the wings off the Rotunda that had escaped my inspection. This was formerly used for a college program. When the program ended, the college left supplies and equipment, including glass jars of specimens in toxic fluid. Since the program was not operating, no one took responsibility for the former classrooms or their contents. The assistant deputy for treatment soon discovered he had a disposal task ahead. I met with department heads and confirmed that every part of the physical plant had a responsible person. We ended up renting dumpsters to get rid of years' worth of accumulated junk. Even if our push for accreditation failed, we had a safer prison as a result of the effort.

Supervisors became skilled at checking caustic and toxic inventories and accounting for critical tools with shadow boards. We replaced some particularly dangerous cleaning supplies with ones less hazardous that required a little more elbow grease to produce results. This was not a problem; we had plenty of workers. The documentation required for the consent decree often transferred to ACA standards nicely. When the pre-audit was done, it appeared we were well prepared. The three days of the actual audit were hard. Some thought malicious staff might deliberately cause us to lose a mandatory standard; however, I did not share that concern. My issue was that auditors bring their own sets of standards in addition to those of the ACA and I worried that some unknown factor would cause us to fail. Fortunately, the few deficiencies the auditors detected were able to be remedied and a recheck found us in compliance. When the auditors left, I was able to gather staff and celebrate our success. We had confounded the naysayers and managed to get the oldest prison in the system accredited. And we would go on to achieve subsequent reaccreditations throughout my time at the facility.

A second initiative came about because I had a researcher at home with time on his hands. I asked Bill to design a survey to measure staff satisfaction at the facility. Bill had retired in part because the agency had become more political, and research was no longer used for making decisions. He was still interested in the business and was willing to help. Staff were a little suspicious about being surveyed; we did not get a particularly good return rate on the 1992 survey, but more responded in 1995, although the numbers dropped off in the final 1998 survey. One part of this process I enjoyed was that staff could ask to discuss their responses with me. Many took the opportunity to do so. While I made it a point to visit all areas of the prison, conversation in the middle of a work site is different than one-on-one in an office. I found the dialogue prompted by the survey process to be valuable in making course corrections.

The next initiative proved to be the most satisfying; it had the most impact on the facility and, later, the department. The National Academy of Corrections, which had already provided me with so many helpful rounds of training, offered a new course called "Cognitive Approaches to Changing Inmate

Behaviors." In November of 1992, Psychologist Jim Conklin, Unit Manager Mark Gassman, Counselor Dave Zarka, and I attended this program. It offered information on three cognitive avenues that research had shown changed prisoner conduct. The one we came away from the session planning to use was called "Skill Training." It was premised on the theory that the use of new skills, ones that the prisoner identified as desiring, would lead to changes in that prisoner's thinking, with the result that the prisoner would be less likely to reoffend. The other possibilities were "Problem Solving" and "Cognitive Restructuring." Even though it was a sick corrections joke that a first-degree murderer was just a bad problem solver, we had rejected that approach as not being broad enough to impact the young and violent men housed at the Reformatory. We thought the cognitive restructuring avenue took too long and was too complicated; we decided we did not have the time or resources to tackle that option.

As we began planning to implement cognitive skill training, we realized that it, too, did not address the significantly warped thinking that our inmates exhibited. Many saw themselves as victims, even though they had raped, robbed, or killed. When asked what their plans were after release, most said they planned to open their own business—even though many had not even graduated high school and came from impoverished backgrounds. They would describe themselves as good people despite histories of violent crimes. As we considered the training we had received, we realized the cognitive restructuring approach was the one most needed by our prisoners.

Looking for a model, we turned to Jack Bush and Brian Billodeau, who were running the Violent Offender Program in the Vermont DOC and who had developed a manual called *Options*. Jack had been one of the academy trainers and, when contacted about a visit to his program, was enthusiastic. Bill and I were vacationing and able to make the trip include Vermont. I was quite impressed with what I saw and asked about a visit from a team from the Reformatory. Again, Jack and Brian were welcoming. The team was as impressed as I had been, and the next move was to ask the National Institute of Corrections to fund a seminar so Reformatory staff could hear from Bush and Billodeau in Michigan. Fortunately, that application was granted, and we had one-and-a-half days of training about the theory of cognitive work with offenders. We held it at Ionia's downtown theatre and invited staff from throughout the DOC. A smaller group, which had volunteered to deliver the program, then had three-and-a-half days of practical, hands-on practice delivering the lessons in *Options*, discussing the kinds of barriers offenders would raise, and the interventions to counteract them.

There were staff, mostly mental health professionals, who thought officers and counselors did not have the educational background to provide this kind of programming. Access to counseling from the few psychologists at the facility was reserved for those nearing release or in acute crisis, so I did not see how the earnest involvement by staff trained in cognitive work could be harmful. The prisoners in the program were all volunteers, and program staff had been cautioned to direct anyone who seemed to be mentally ill to the mental health team.

Although the program was nominally under the direction of the assistant deputy warden for Housing, it was actually overseen by a steering committee made up of a unit manager, involved counselors and officers, and the warden. We named the program "Strategies for Thinking Productively" (STP). The team approach was encouraged by the academy training and did seem to be the best way to manage the effort. Prisoners with violent crimes were given priority for inclusion. The introductory session was called Phase I and involved fourteen lessons delivered in sixteen sessions over an eight-week period. The DOC agreed this would qualify as group counseling, so offenders were happy to participate. Those who wished to continue into Phase II had to agree to stay at the Reformatory for up to two years to complete that part. For those wishing to continue to consolidate the changes they had begun in Phase II, a final Phase III was available.

The premise of all cognitive programs is that how you think controls how you behave. In cognitive restructuring, prisoners identify behavior they want to change and then determine the attitudes and beliefs supporting that behavior. Several mechanisms can be used for behavior change, including thought stopping, but the most enduring is the replacement of old attitudes and beliefs with new ones that support desired new behavior.

As planning began for Phase II implementation, we had an opportunity to create a residential component. As a result of consent decree physical plant changes, segregation was being moved to the outside of I Block. That made the Adjustment Center space available. It was the right size, just under eighty beds; however, it was in the oldest part of the facility. The cells were smaller than others in the general population and the space seemed more oppressive. On the plus side, there were adjacent group rooms, a small activity area/ dayroom, and a separate outdoor exercise area with space for a garden. The steering committee decided this would be the program's home. We let the prisoners pick the colors for their cells—from available institutional paint— and added a microwave to the dayroom as incentives. Program participants acknowledged that living with other men who were trying to do the hard work of self-change was beneficial.

Phase II began in 1994. It involved group meetings of up to eight prisoners with two staff as observers. Each group was structured around a thinking report of a single prisoner and lasted about an hour. The featured prisoner presented a situation that got him into trouble and all the thoughts and feelings he could recall during the event. He also noted the attitudes and beliefs he identified as supporting the thinking. His fellow prisoners then asked him questions to help him clarify or find additional thoughts and feelings. Sometimes they suggested he identify additional beliefs or attitudes he had not considered. The presenting prisoner was always the final arbiter, though, about the thinking report's contents. Staff were there to keep order, keep the questioning respectful and on target, and, in the long term, to determine whether the prisoners were doing the hard work of self-change and assisting others toward that goal.

For program integrity, groups were periodically audited. I had the privilege of auditing when a prisoner had his lightbulb moment. "I like to hurt people," he said. I wish I could describe his tone—it seemed to contain revulsion, self-knowledge, and wonder. That epiphany spurred him to read everything we had in the program library and to redouble his efforts at change. Through thinking reports and journal activity he also recalled being sexually assaulted by an uncle as a youngster. (This prompted a referral to the mental health team.) While his current crime was nonviolent, one of his previous crimes was directing the sexual assault of another prisoner in the county jail. To move from Phase II to Phase III, prisoners had to offer a thinking report on their crime. This prisoner could have chosen the nonviolent current offense, but instead presented about the sexual assault. When staff asked him why he made that choice, he responded that it was the one with the behavior he most wanted to change.

We were clear that he liked to hurt people. He had what looked like marbles at the joint of his jaws because he so often clenched his teeth to avoid hitting someone. Most staff stayed a clear arm's length away from him because we knew what a short fuse he had. It was unusual for him to be out of segregation for longer than a few months because of his explosive temper. He managed to avoid violent misconduct while in the program and was able to move to reduced custody at another prison. I have always thought of him as the offender who accomplished the most significant change while in the program.

An additional element of Phase II was journaling. Each prisoner was charged with keeping track of his daily efforts to change and to review the journal with a staff partner weekly. This was complicated by some offenders' near illiteracy, but those who wanted to be in the program had to find a way to handle all the requirements. From a security perspective, journaling was the most troubling. While we wanted prisoners to have privacy for what could be difficult discussions, we needed to be able to see that staff members were safe during those meetings. Fortunately, most offices we used had windows and were well lit. Only on one occasion was a staff person at risk and the prisoner involved had absorbed enough of the program's goals that he confessed his intentions before carrying out his plan.

He had, however, managed to get as far as putting together a kit designed to immobilize his female journal partner. He had planned a murder/suicide based on a movie he had watched. Over time, he had developed feelings for the journal partner. He understood that she did not return these feelings, but had decided if he could not have her, no one else would either. No one had detected his inappropriate attraction and it was only his confession that averted a tragedy. I counted it as a win for the program, but the prisoner had to go to maximum security with relevant misconduct reports, even though he had done the right thing by letting staff know his plan.

When staff felt a prisoner needed a course correction, a meeting called a "Treatment Team" would be held. These would be triggered if thinking reports were not ready for the group or participation was lacking when others were presenting thinking reports. Failure to journal consistently or to acknowledge thinking errors would be other reasons for a Treatment Team meeting. Unit officers, program staff, and the journal partner would meet with the prisoner to clarify expectations, describe how the prisoner was not meeting these, and determine his willingness to participate. Usually, offenders decided to continue with an improved attitude; however, Treatment Team meetings occasionally resulted in the prisoner leaving the program.

»»»»»»»»»»»

In 1995, I was asked to be on the faculty for a NIC-sponsored training called "Strategies for Success for Women Who are Wardens." This was held in Cincinnati, Ohio, and brought together women from around the Midwest. What was most memorable for me at this session was watching networks form and personal relationships develop. I had known Michigan's Pat Caruso and found Ohio's Melody Turner a kindred spirit. Both women became NAAWS members as well as personal friends. They also were instrumental in the success of the final grand adventure of this phase of my time at the Reformatory.

In the pursuit of professional development, I attended a Women Working in Corrections and Juvenile Justice conference in Pittsburgh in the spring of 1995. While there, I spoke with Joann Morton and others about the mechanics of creating these conferences when there was no organization to support them. She and those who had hosted in the past gave me the confidence to suggest Michigan as a good site for the next gathering, which would be in the fall of 1996. Beginning with Perry Johnson and continuing under Directors Bob Brown and Ken McGinnis, the Michigan DOC had developed a strong cadre of women, many in leadership positions. Before confirming the offer, though, I called Director McGinnis, who agreed to provide some in-kind resources if I could figure out how to manage the funding for the event. I also made sure Luella Burke would agree to cochair. Finally, I called the Amway Grand Plaza Hotel in Grand Rapids and booked the conference for October 13-16, 1996, using my personal credit card. I had worked with the hotel's convention manager when hosting a Michigan Corrections Association Conference and knew the facility was superior and the staff would ensure attendees had an excellent experience.

What kind of crazy person will put their personal finances at risk like that? In my case, one who has seen the power of women with a mission. I knew Luella was a master at picking the right people for the roles necessary to create a successful conference. We managed to convince the Michigan Corrections Association and the Michigan Sheriffs' Association to join Women Police of Michigan and the Michigan Department of Corrections as sponsors for the conference. The sponsors had no responsibility for funding the event, but their involvement offered the possibility of in-kind resources. These did later materialize. The DOC offered vans and drivers for facility tours, authorized administrative leave and training credits, and strongly encouraged supervisors to send employees to the conference. The sheriffs' association helped with security, MCA offered committee members who had experience with conference planning and execution, and WPM provided a much-needed fund repository.

Luella got Lurline Baker-Kent and Alethea Taylor Camp to cochair the program committee. Both had national reputations and were able to recruit speakers and create workshop topics of interest to potential attendees. They were assisted by Darlene Schimmel and Nancy Zang from the DOC and Marlys Schujter from the Department of Social Services. Speakers included Margaret Moore, director of the Washington, DC, DOC; Laurie O. Robinson, assistant attorney general of the US Department of Justice; Reginald Wilkerson, president of ACA and director of the Ohio DOC; Sharon Johnson Rion, director of international operations of the Corrections Corporation of America; Morris Thigpen, director, National Institute of Corrections; Harold Clark, director, Nebraska DOC; Elaine Little, director, North Dakota DOC; Flora Boyd, director, South Carolina Department of Juvenile Justice; Gwendolyn Chunn, director, Division of Youth Services, North Carolina Department of Human Resources; Sally Chandler Halford, director, Iowa DOC; Gothriel Silafluer, commissioner, Minnesota DOC; Judy Uphoff, director, Wyoming DOC; Dora B. Schriro, director, Missouri DOC; Susan Hunter, chief of the Prisons Division, National Institute of Corrections; George Lynch, president, National Association of Blacks in Criminal Justice; and Michigan's current director of corrections, Ken McGinnis, and former directors Perry Johnson and Bob Brown.

Most of the other committee chairs were from Michigan. Nancy Gassman handled finance and partnered with Women Police of Michigan, which had a nonprofit tax ID number. Jeri Ann Sherry later joined that committee. With WPM handling the money, we did not need to work around a cumbersome state bureaucracy to pay the bills. Pat Caruso and Melody Turner of Ohio recruited vendors and found advertisers. Both were well known by ACA vendors and they used ACA conferences to push for support of our conference. They were assisted by Marta Villacorta of Florida, Susan Cranford of Texas, and Rukhsanna Akran of Ohio.

Public relations was primarily handled by Marsha Foresman with a DOC public information staffer as cochair. He recruited Lansing TV personality Sheri Jones, who turned out to be a good connection to other media outlets. Judy Anderson of South Carolina was the national representative on that committee, and Deb Wieber and Bill Overton also assisted. Bobbi Butler, Noreen Sawatzki, and Bob Jenson headed local arrangements, assisted by Miguel Berrios and Marion Palmer. They created an opening-night reception at the Gerald Ford Museum, a casino night at the Amway, and a trip to Lake Michigan with dinner at a restaurant overlooking the lake. They also provided information about Grand Rapids as part of the program materials.

Registration was the responsibility of Carol Frederick and Dinah Johnson Moore, with help from Mark Coulter, Sharee Booker, and Jeff VanderGalien. Ionia County Sheriff Terry Jungel chaired security, Val Chaplin produced the printed program with help from the Ionia Temporary Facility Print Shop, and Sue Coley and Ruth Smith coordinated special meals.

After more than a year of meeting and planning, the conference was finally about to start. The Amway gave me a lovely suite the night before the conference began. I planned to take Bill there and enjoy his company before things got busy. While wrapping up conference details, I had also made an inquiry of Dan Bolden, who was head of Michigan's prisons. Bob Lecureux was retiring from Kinross in Sault Ste. Marie. Bill had often expressed a desire to live in the UP and I had done ten years at the Reformatory, so I asked if I might be moved to Kinross. When I discussed this with Bill later, he was horrified. "I don't want to live in that godforsaken swamp," he said. By the UP, he had meant Marquette and west, which he regarded as the beautiful part of Michigan. I immediately contacted the deputy director's office and withdrew my request. Bolden responded through my immediate supervisor, JoAnn Bach, that I would be in the Soo (Sault Ste. Marie) "before the snow flies." Oh boy. If I told Bill about this, my hope for a romantic overnight at the Amway would be toast. On the other hand, I was ordinarily honest with him. My body resolved the problem for me by shutting down my vocal cords. I simply could not speak. I had not been ill and had no explanation except that the loss of speech was psychosomatic. It solved the problem of telling Bill we were going to Kinross (or at least I was). Unfortunately, it also reduced me to writing responses to the myriad questions that arose during the ensuing conference. When Bolden showed up at the event, I cornered him right away. I wrote that Bill would not go to Kinross and I did not want to go there alone. He just laughed and told me that Bill had played so many jokes on others over the years that he (Bolden) thought he would pay him back. I did not have to go to Kinross after all. And it was me, not Bill, who suffered from Bolden's joke.

The conference was a huge success. Over eight hundred women and men from around the country participated. At least twenty states and eight Michigan counties were represented in addition to Michigan Department of Corrections employees. The weather cooperated with unseasonable warmth and sun. Men who attended had the unusual experience of being in the minority, which created some discomfort. This was especially true after Margaret Moore, one of the major presenters, was characteristically frank about her and others' negative experiences at the hands of male coworkers. After her remarks, I got to practice de-escalation techniques I had learned for prisoner interactions with a male colleague from the Reformatory. He was finally able to depersonalize the speaker's comments, but it took a while. The excitement and energy were wonderful. Luella and I felt we had made Michigan proud. Best of all, we were able to meet expenses and have $40,000 left over. Half went to Nebraska, the next state hosting the WWICJJ conference, for a nice startup fund. The rest was given to the DOC for scholarships for individuals from Michigan to attend the WWICJJ in Nebraska.

That middle five years had gone fast, and we had accomplished much. I could hardly wait to see what the next years would bring.

»»»»»»»»»»»»

Lesson Learned: Take big bites. Attempt accreditation even though it seems like a long shot. Start an evidence-based program with minimal agency support.

Corrections Story: I was talking with staff and prisoners near the recreation yard one evening when I overheard one prisoner tell another, "She's the one who flamed that prisoner down in Jackson, you know." That had been years ago, and I was initially disturbed to think that some prisoners saw me as a person who would knowingly light up an offender. On the other hand, some thought I was too easy on those in my care, so I guess this was a way to keep my reputation balanced.

9. THE REFORMATORY: FINAL YEARS

The final five years at Michigan Reformatory were wonderful and awful. During the first five years, getting the place under control was the goal. The next period involved changing the organization's culture: no more physical abuse of prisoners; policy compliance and professional standards of conduct were the norm; and programming to offer prisoners the opportunity to change. I envisioned ending my career consolidating these gains.

In 1996, with several years of cognitive work at the Reformatory completed, I went to the NIC Academy in Colorado to help present a seminar about cognitive work. Reformatory staff continued to provide training in Michigan for our own employees as well as those from other prisons. Occasionally, someone from another state would ask to attend; we hosted participants from Wisconsin, Ohio, and Indiana. John Bergman with the Geese Theatre Company came to the Reformatory to teach us to use role playing in group work. I signed the manifest to allow Tosser, his small, curly-haired, white dog, to go to the chapel for training, although custody staff clearly thought this was a bad idea. While some offenders seemed leery of the animal, others were excited to pet and hold it. Therapy animals in prisons were not yet common, but I could see where these might be useful. STP continued to be a positive element at the prison. When asked to deliver training at the Oaks Correctional Facility in Manistee and Hiawatha Correctional Facility in Sault Ste. Marie, we were delighted to travel to spread the good news about cognitive work with offenders.

Prison life can be brutal, and I got a taste of that in 1997. We had been working hard to keep metal weapons out of the hands of prisoners. That effort saved an officer's life. When prisoners fashioned a shank (prison-made weapon) for assaulting a targeted officer, the only material they could find was the kind of aluminum edging you might find around a kitchen table. The assailant stabbed the officer in the chest, but his sternum bent the blade and he survived. Two other staff were injured coming to his assistance. A prisoner inside a housing unit was seen giving a signal of success to others on the yard. We had a system to monitor inmate phone calls and, soon after the signal was given, heard a prisoner say, "We got him." That told us the assault was part of a coordinated plan.

We locked the prison down for several days and conducted searches for weapons and other contraband. Teachers and other non-custody staff delivered bag meals to prisoners in their cells. Slowly, we returned to normal operations, although it was a tense time. I sought counseling because I had been warned repeatedly about the targeted officer's petty abuses of prisoners. He did not physically harm anyone, but he would not give showers when scheduled or would hold a man in his cell until all others had left for chow. There are many ways an officer can abuse his power, and, even though I had asked the officer's supervisors to counsel with him, and had even talked with him myself, he continued to treat prisoners badly. While I cannot justify the actions of the prisoners, I understand that they had tried legitimate methods to resolve the problems the officer was causing them and, in their minds, the action they took was needed. The reason I turned to counseling was to come to terms with the staff injuries I had been unable to prevent and, ultimately, to confront the fact that I could not ensure the safety of those in my care.

One good thing did come out of this incident. Because of information gathered after the assault, I was able to make a case for shutting down a religious group called the Melanic Islamic Palace of the Rising Sun. We felt this was more of a gang than a religion and had been keeping a close eye on them. Unlike most religious groups, this one had no counterpart in the free world. It was a prisoner-made-up religion based loosely on the tenets of the Koran. Even the other Islamic groups, the Moorish Science Temple of America, and Nation of Islam, seemed to be wary of Melanics, who had a reputation for recklessness and violence. When I met with the group's leader and explained that they would no longer be permitted to meet pending review from the DOC director, the news was not well accepted. In fact, it was reported that the group put out a hit on me and Deputy Renico. At the request of custody supervisors, I stayed out of the chow hall for a few days and avoided wandering around the prison during times of prisoner movement, but soon returned to my usual practices and never came to harm.

Of course, there were also good things happening at the Reformatory. By June of 1996, there were eight Phase I STP groups inside the facility and two at the dorm. Five Phase II groups were operating in the old Adjustment Center, now called G-Block. By January 1997, two prisoners had moved into Phase III, with two waiting to be interviewed to make that move. It was not until the fall of 1997 that five prisoners were in Phase III. That was the maximum number in that status during the program. The primary reason was that prisoners' positive conduct while in the program resulted in their eligibility for reduced custody. We encouraged men to move on when they had completed Phase II and were eligible to step down in custody level. Not only was that a good test of their commitment to change, but it also freed space at the Reformatory for prisoners who needed the structure and security we provided.

For those who did stay on for Phase III, we provided journal partners and socializing activities. One I initiated was a weekly warden's dinner. I brought in silverware, plates, glasses and even cloth place mats and napkins. Up to eight individuals were able to dine at a time, so I invited staff involved in STP, and sometimes staff critical of the program, to join us in a group room near G-Block. We began the meal, which was the same food being served in the chow hall, with a moment of silence. Then serving bowls and platters were passed and conversation ensued. Afterward, the prisoners did the dishes while I was responsible for counting and locking up the silverware, plates, and glasses. There was some discussion about the need to learn about place settings and the niceties of dining, but the prisoners accepted my explanation that it was preparation for when they were released and took a young lady out to dinner. Because most seemed unfamiliar with dining family style, I asked about that. I was told that sitting around a table to eat just was not done, even for holidays. When they were hungry, their mom just gave them some money and they went to the corner store.

»»»»»»»»»»»»

Even though research into cognitive programs has confirmed their efficacy, I wrote to colleges and universities within driving distance of the Reformatory and solicited researchers to validate our version. Dr. Agnes Baro of Grand Valley State University had agreed to conduct research on the STP program. Because of the voluntary nature of STP, we identified prisoners for a control group from other self-help programs such as AA/NA, religious groups, or school. The researchers selected a random group from this pool. Dr. Baro looked at the behavior of both Phase I and Phase II participants as compared to the controls, all of whom had been in programs for at least eight weeks. To my surprise, Phase I prisoners showed a statistically significant reduction in disobeying a direct order (DDO) misconducts. In Phase II, the reduction in DDO continued and there was also a statistically significant reduction in misconduct for assault. Since DDO was the most frequently occurring misconduct in all prisons in Michigan, a reduction was important. Also, DDO events sometimes escalate into more serious misconduct. I think anyone would agree that fewer assaults in prison is also desirable. In the case of prisoners serving a term of years, the timekeeping system automatically added a week to the offender's sentence every month in which a misconduct occurred. Reduction in misconduct translated to earlier eligibility for parole, which could mean a savings for the taxpayer. We celebrated the good news brought by Dr. Baro's research.

In addition to evaluating prisoners involved in STP, Dr. Baro and a graduate assistant, Scott Scheidmantel, looked at staff. Their research was titled "STP Participation and Job Satisfaction, Work Stress, and Life Stress: A Comparison of Correctional Workers at the Michigan Reformatory." An anonymous survey was the research tool, with specially coded numbers identifying twenty-one of the four hundred surveys. Those twenty-one were from individuals who had worked with the STP program for at least a year. The return rate on the survey was 63.8 percent, which was considered quite good when compared to other research conducted on correctional employees. A control group, matched by age, gender, education, job type, and correctional experience (both at the Reformatory and in the DOC), was identified. The sole significant difference for STP workers was lower work stress. Job satisfaction and life stress were about the same between those who worked in the STP program and in other areas of the prison. I had hoped that job satisfaction would be higher for those working in the program. Perhaps it was not because participating in an activity seen by many as "soft" would limit the positive experience. It was good, however, to know that staff were not being harmed by working in STP and some were benefitting.

Elements of the consent decree continued to be challenges, especially adequate out-of-cell time. I suggested we merge consent decree requirements and STP efforts by developing an involuntary cognitive program. The research told us that men who sought to change improved in two key misconduct areas. Could compelled cognitive exposure also have a positive effect on conduct? Director McGinnis agreed that prisoners who screened Level V (maximum security) could be assigned to the program, even if that required transfer to the Reformatory. Ferris State University agreed to conduct the research this time. The legislature funded additional officer and case manager positions so that we could expand the number of groups and journal partners.

It was exciting to plan a new program. We continued to use the steering committee to guide this effort. To recruit corrections officers, we worked with the union to create new housing officer positions with weekends off and 8:00-4:00 shifts. Existing case managers were asked whether they wanted to work in the cognitive unit before new staff were hired. We remodeled space in one of the wings off the Rotunda for group rooms and staff offices. To differentiate this program from STP, we brainstormed and came up with CHANGE, the acronym standing for Cognitive Housing Approach: New Goals Environment. The inside of I Block was designated as the housing space for participants and we began moving prisoners into the program.

In discussing the research design with the Ferris team, we decided on a pre/post evaluation. In other words, we would look at the prisoners' behaviors for a period before program participation and then again for the same period after completion. One element I stressed to the team was a research structure that would permit individual prisoner behavior to be the key. I anticipated that a few inmates would simply refuse to participate, receiving a DDO misconduct daily, and did not want the behavior of a knucklehead or two to be aggregated with what we hoped would be improved conduct for most. The research team split their duties so that two came to the facility to monitor group sessions and the third crunched the numbers.

Not surprisingly, prisoners selected for the CHANGE program were hostile. They resisted moving to I Block or coming to the Reformatory. All needed to complete their GED (high school equivalency), so were assigned to school and most went to that program willingly. Attending groups for cognitive work was a different story. Staff got high marks for their ability to persuade most to give it a try. About the time we were starting CHANGE, the National Institute of Corrections developed a new manual, called *Thinking for a Change*, which combined lessons for cognitive self-change, problem solving, and skill training. We decided to shift gears and use this new resource. Additional training for those offering the new lessons was needed, so we scheduled and delivered it. Some staff liked the old *Options* format better and remained focused on STP; however, over time, STP lessons shifted to the new manual.

For the skill-training lessons, prisoners were given small blue cards with the steps of the skill listed. Staff reported that, for skills like "Asking a Question" or "Having a Difficult Conversation," they would observe prisoners consulting their cards before engaging. It is hard to imagine needing cue cards for these basic skills, but if your way of getting what you want has been violence or the threat of violence, you probably did not develop the skills most pro-social people take for granted. CHANGE staff felt prisoners were adapting to the program and many were making positive changes. We waited for the Ferris research to confirm that belief.

»»»»»»»»»»»»

We ended 1997 with no dorm escapes. This was the first year in memory for that achievement, and it was a significant milestone. That same year we had University of Michigan students provide a theatre workshop. After lengthy negotiations with the DOC technology specialists, computers for prisoners were installed in the renovated H-Ward school. In 1998, Paul Renico was promoted to the St. Louis warden's job and I hired Lee Gilman, who served as deputy until I retired.

We began to hold formal GED graduation ceremonies to which prisoners' families were invited. These were held in the visiting rooms and the Prisoner Benefit Fund paid for refreshments as well as caps and gowns for the graduates. The ceremonies were videotaped and broadcast on the internal cable channel, with each graduate given a brief period to speak if they wanted. Most did; I have letters from men who were grateful for having that special experience with their families. For some, it was the first time they had celebrated a positive event.

»»»»»»»»»»»

We continued the STP/CHANGE programs and I was the journal partner with an STP participant, Ron Hammond. He was serving a life sentence with no possibility of parole for a particularly cold-blooded murder committed during a carjacking when he was only seventeen. Although he was clearly bright, he was also manipulative and resistant to change. His intellectual abilities let him offer all the right responses; however, my staff and I thought he was going to be one of our challenges. Thus, I agreed to be his journal partner. That meant I met with him weekly in Phase III while he worked on the changes he had targeted. These were pride, refusal to listen, verbal abuse, dehumanizing, physical aggression, and refusing to admit being wrong. During our journaling sessions, we discussed society's attitudes toward crime and punishment. As I had told other prisoners, I shared that I had observed a pendulum moving from rehabilitation to "lock 'em up and throw away the key." We were in the latter phase, having opened a "punk prison" in Michigan operated by a private-prison company and finding the system in constant need of additional beds to meet an influx of prisoners. I thought that pendulum would return to support prisoner reformation, and he needed to maintain a good record in the event he ever became eligible for commutation. His record supported a move to reduced custody, and, although he initially resisted that change, he finally agreed and was moved to a level II prison where he lived in one of the pole barns I have described.

He wrote to me twice while I was still a warden. The first time, he thanked me for bringing the STP program to the Reformatory and expressed hope that he could manage without that structure, even offering to help set up a similar program at his new prison. The second letter was from an Upper Peninsula prison where he had been transferred after being involved in making and selling wine. He justified that conduct, citing the loss of income he had experienced when transferred. I agreed to help him connect with a staff person who might be a Phase III journal partner if he could manage a transfer to a downstate prison where STP-trained staff were available. That was my last contact with Mr. Hammond as a warden.

»»»»»»»»»»»

In 1998, Ferris State University asked me to join their criminal justice advisory board. Like the other advisory boards, it met quarterly. The difference was that other areas of law enforcement were represented. That offered some opportunities for fruitful discussions about offenders, and I found that I enjoyed these meetings immensely.

Another activity that year was preparing for reaccreditation. As in the past, I roamed the facility, looking for areas which might present problems if seen by the auditors. Two incidents are memorable. The recreation supervisors' office desk and storage space yielded felt markers considered toxic that were contraband, as well as a stash of prisoner tokens (prison money). There was no reason for a staff person to have the latter. The markers were permitted if accounted for as a toxic/caustic material. The absence of such a record could have caused us to fail a mandatory standard. While experience suggested we would have had a chance to rectify this problem in an actual audit, I was particularly unhappy because the responsible employee was one of the star STP providers. I felt betrayed by his disregard of the rules, even though my rational brain understood there was not anything personal about the violation. I left a note that the items could be claimed in the warden's office and took them to the shift commander to be manifested out of the facility.

The second situation involved the Michigan State Industries sergeant. This position was coveted because the hours were 8:00—4:00, Monday through Friday. The job was to ensure security measures were in place at the industrial laundry and furniture factory. In addition, it monitored activities at the inside maintenance building. This must have not been a full-time job because, in most cases, the MSI sergeant would eventually be removed due to some sort of foolishness. My involvement was the discovery, when shaking down the office of the sergeant, of a stash of skin magazines (all addressed to prisoners) as well as various contraband items including tools with the identifying numbers obliterated. Again, I left a message identifying what I had taken, although not offering to return them this time. I carried a box containing these finds across the yard to the shift commander's office. Since it appeared the tools with obliterated numbers might be headed out of the facility, I suggested the shift commander investigate their source. The magazines were to be delivered to their rightful owners or destroyed. Just as with the markers, the proper accounting for the tools was part of a mandatory standard and failure could have foiled our quest for reaccreditation. I like to think my example of taking a hard look, even at people and places thought to be compliant, helped us achieve that final reaccreditation.

»»»»»»»»»»»»»

On a fall weekend in 1998, an officer took a pair of trusted prisoners into the inside maintenance building to clean. In an escape attempt, they knocked him out, took his keys and radio, and left him locked in a tool crib. He came to and found the only window without bars in the building and escaped through it, injuring a leg in the process, but managed to alert other staff. The prisoners were still in the building and one took the other hostage, but let him surrender after a brief period. Then the remaining prisoner attempted suicide by cutting his own throat. By that time, a squad had been deployed; I was on site and ordered gas to be administered to prevent the guy from seriously harming himself. While the DOC had trained hostage negotiators, this incident proceeded too quickly to use those resources. I do not think the escape was well-planned and doubt that it would have been successful; however, the incident was another reminder that prisoners are always looking for a way out, and we cannot become trusting or complacent.

»»»»»»»»»»»»»

At the end of that year, I went to Texas for warden peer interaction training. This was an initiative by Sam Houston State University and involved wardens from around the country. The Texas DOC supported the training by permitting visits to their prisons, including an execution site. I loved the training. Wardens were asked to present what they regarded as a best practice from their agency. This was followed by questions and suggestions from their peers. It was a great opportunity to share ideas and strategies and learn from each other. On the other hand, the practices in the Texas prisons seemed archaic, and I was horrified that they were proud of the efficiency offered by side-by-side electric chairs. Michigan has never had the death penalty. I knew it was expensive to administer and research suggested it was ineffective as a deterrent. My conversations with wardens who had presided over executions also convinced me there was a human toll for prison workers who were involved in the taking of another's life, even if it was done under the color of law.

»»»»»»»»»»»»»

The next year, we foiled an escape plot in the winter. Prisoners had stolen kitchen whites (white uniforms for prisoner workers) so they would blend in with the snow after going over the wall. That was to be accomplished with thirty-seven feet of plastic netting that had been used to secure a crumbling dry kiln, furniture pads, boots, and gloves. The netting was to be used to get to the top of the wall. The pads, boots, and gloves were to defeat the razor wire above the wall. Fortunately, none of the equipment the co-conspirators had acquired was used, except as evidence of their plot. They did get out of the Reformatory—but it was to a maximum-security facility.

»»»»»»»»»»»»

Sometime during the last few years, we had a torrential rainstorm. A stream that ran through the property became a torrent which carried a large tree and smashed a sewer line that ran under the bridge to the shooting range. The damage was discovered quickly. Because I was living in the area, I knew the city of Ionia was replacing sewer lines and had the equipment and supplies needed for repairs. I called a friend from the Business and Professional Women's Club who worked for Ionia's public works department. She was dismayed at the idea of raw sewage from the Ionia Maximum Security Facility and the Michigan Training Unit running into the Grand River and dispatched a truck with two workers and the needed pipe replacement. I had, by the time they arrived, called my boss and alerted her to the problem. Before people from DOC's Emergency Preparedness and the Department of Natural Resources's Environmental Quality sections could get to the facility, my staff and the city's crew had the line replaced. This was a time that local knowledge and connections really paid off.

»»»»»»»»»»»»

Speaking of networking, I had the honor of emceeing the retirement of Marge VanOchten, the feminist voice of corrections during my time with the department. She served as legal counsel for the agency and attended wardens' meetings, executive staff meetings, and oversaw litigation, including the consent decree. In an environment that was still getting used to women as peers, she often was the lightning rod for women's rights. Many men in the business feared her sharp tongue and acerbic wit. Bill liked her and I loved the fact that she was willing to be the voice for women in corrections. In our agency, most retirement parties turn out to be roasts with way too much drinking. My recollection is that hers was more celebratory and less drunken. In any event, she sent a lovely thank-you note afterward.

In July of 2000, I had just had my first sip of after-dinner brandy when the phone rang. About fifty prisoners were refusing to return to their cells after yard time. They were upset about a new yard schedule and wanted vending machines in the visiting room. I called my boss, JoAnn Bach, and told her about the incident, confessed I had had a sip of hooch, and suggested that I go to the prison anyway. I certainly was not impaired and felt comfortable dealing with the situation. She concurred and I headed back to work. The shift commanders and I discussed our response. We had armed officers on the roof, had removed staff from the yard, and had supervisors talking with the ringleaders. Squads with helmets, shields, and batons were being formed in case the prisoners tried to leave the fenced yard; however, these were kept out of the prisoners' view. Some staff wanted to use the squads and force the prisoners into segregation. Since everyone was safe, I preferred to wait them out. The Reformatory was near the Grand River and there was plenty of marshy ground that bred huge mosquitos. As night fell, these winged predators would descend on the yard and make it quite unpleasant.

I reviewed files of the self-appointed leaders and identified a few I knew and thought would be reasonable. These men were brought to an office adjacent to the Rotunda. While Sgt. Pat Kelley monitored their behavior, I listened respectfully to their complaints. Then I told them we were already planning to add vending machines for the visiting room and prisoners needed to be patient while we found and installed them. The yard schedule was not going to change. They took in this information, shook hands with me, and returned to the yard. We gave them a while to share the information and then directed all the prisoners back to their unit. Participants were searched and admitted in groups of three without further incident. Some were later transferred to maximum security with incite-to-riot misconduct violations.

Soon after that incident, Ferris presented their preliminary evaluation of the CHANGE program, and it was not good. Their report suggested that participation was not only failing to result in improved conduct, it was actually harming prisoners by creating more misconduct. Even though this information conflicted with staff reports of prisoner participants' increased self-control and attempts at change, I elected to believe the numbers. I shared the research with the director and suggested we end the program. He agreed. Several years after I had retired, I spotted an article in *Corrections Today*, the American Correctional Association's magazine, which claimed the program was a success. It did not name the Reformatory (citing a Midwestern prison), but the author was the numbers cruncher from Ferris. The program's description made it clear it was about CHANGE. Although I was angry and upset when I saw it, I did not contact the author. Either he lied to us initially or fudged the numbers when cognitive work became more common and acceptable. It made no difference at that point because the program no longer existed.

The year ended with another new program, "Prisoners Who Care, Read." This was the brainchild of literacy volunteer Mary Ann Hagermeyer. She had been working with low-level readers and wanted to find a way to reward them for reaching literacy goals. She got funding to purchase children's books that prisoners read and recorded. The book and recording were then mailed to or given to the offenders' children during a visit. What a great way to encourage reading and model good parenting. I was happy to partner with her on that effort.

»»»»»»»»»»»»

Although we do not often admit it, wardens have favorite staff. In my case, a pair who had grown significantly due to their involvement in the STP effort made that list. Deb Davis was a corrections officer who sometimes created problems. Her work was fine. Her choice of paramours was not. The coworkers she paired up with were often abusive, and, when she came to work with the inevitable black eye or bruised cheek, staff would take sides. The drama was just not conducive to productive work. When she volunteered for STP, I was not sure I wanted the potential disruption, but decided to include her anyway. She said that decision was a turning point in her life. She used what she learned about changing thinking to change behavior and applied the processes to her own life. As she grew and changed, she became a role model for other staff. Her personal life smoothed out and she reports she still uses the techniques when facing challenges. When she retired from the state, she transitioned to work for Ionia County, delivering cognitive programs at the jail and to probationers.

The other person is Abe French, who was an officer when he became involved in STP. He enjoyed the work, went to college, and completed his degree. As a result, he qualified for a case manager's job and I was happy to hire him in that role. He was later promoted to a job in Central Office and charged with deciding what programs in the state would receive budgeted funding for jails and community corrections. Like Deb, he feels that participation in cognitive work had a significant positive effect on his life. After he retired, he developed training in cognitive programming and delivers this across Michigan, as well as providing consultant services to other jurisdictions.

And, of course, I was a beneficiary of cognitive work. Because of the programs the Reformatory initiated, Grand Valley State University held a convocation in 2000 and presented me with an honorary doctor of laws degree. This was a lovely occasion attended by family and friends. My son, John, was eloquent in a TV interview following the ceremony. Then, in May of 2001, Ferris State followed suit and gave me an honorary doctor of public service degree. The North American Association of Wardens and Superintendents selected me as warden of the year, with the celebration scheduled in August at the ACA conference in Philadelphia.

Unknown to all except my bosses, I had been planning to retire. Keeping this quiet was important because as soon as staff know you are leaving, your authority diminishes. I had hoped to leave without much fuss; however, staff insisted that there be a party. I did not want a formal affair and especially did not want alcohol served—that encourages bad behavior. The compromise was a pig roast in June on prison grounds. The weather cooperated and I was delighted when friends came from near and far to celebrate. Bill presented me with a cookbook and an apron, announcing that he was done being the chief cook. Director Bill Martin brought the obligatory proclamation from the legislature along with leadership and meritorious service awards. Administrative Assistant Robbin Bell created a lovely scrapbook with photos from the event and gave me a pair of huge retirement cards signed by many staff. John and his wife, Kris, brought me to tears with their gift—a small silver frame with the message: "Coming to you in 2002." I was to get my first local grandchild in January. And that was how I transitioned from prison warden to private citizen.

»»»»»»»»»»»»

Lesson Learned: In reflecting on the prison years, an insight about prisoners surfaced. While formal prisoner classifications systems often focus on a prisoner's dangerousness, length of sentence, need for academic and vocational training, substance abuse treatment programs, and mental and physical health treatment, I classify prisoners in a different way. In my experience, offenders can usually be thought of as sad, mad, or bad. By sad, I mean they may have cognitive deficits due to drug or alcohol use by their mother while pregnant, abuse as a child, head injuries, malnutrition, or ingestion of lead or other environmental toxins. Sad because they were led into criminal activity by peers or older youth who took advantage of their need to belong. Sad because substance abuse led to criminal acts. Sad because they have no coping skills other than anger and violence. And sad because their untreated mental illness was a factor in their criminality. This group represents most of those who are incarcerated.

Prisoners I call mad are aware they drew a short straw in life. They see no way out of their impoverished and deprived situation other than through criminal activity. Often, they are bright and capable, but have no vision of a better life and often believe they are fated to die young. This group is small, but often creates problems for prison administrators because they foment discontent. The good news is that offenders in this group have the most potential for a fulfilled life when released if they elect to focus on self-change while incarcerated.

The bad group is small in numbers. I can recall a handful of prisoners that I considered irredeemable, but life with no possibility of parole is a good approach that will keep us safe from these men who have no boundaries and no wish to conform to society's rules.

Corrections Story: One day while I was watching evening yard, a prisoner approached me and asked if we could talk. I said yes, and he said he had a question. He noted that at other prisons where he had lived, the warden was always accompanied by "suits" when touring (by this, he meant other high-ranking prison officials). He noted that I usually was alone when moving around the prison and wanted to know why. I told him that I had found that both staff and prisoners were more likely to talk freely with me when I was alone. I showed him the batch of three-by-five cards I carried and told him I made notes of questions or concerns and then was able to follow up later to be sure these were addressed. He indicated he understood and went on about his business.

A few weeks later, I was observing lines in the chow hall. As men passed me, many complained about the meal they had been served. When all prisoners had their food, I went to the line and asked for a tray, receiving the same food as the prisoners. Then I sat at one of the inmate tables and sampled the meal, finding it bland, but palatable. The same prisoner I had spoken with in the yard was working in the dining room. He came over to the table and asked me what I was doing. I explained I was checking the food because of prisoner complaints. He looked pained and said, "Warden, I understood what you told me about going around without suits, but Warden, you have other people who could check on the food. You don't have to eat this s—." I assured him it was the best way I knew how to confirm the meal was acceptable, but admit I left him shaking his head. (This was Bill's favorite story about my work in prisons.)

10. LIFE AFTER CORRECTIONS

People asked me what I planned to do after retirement. I usually responded, "Clean closets." That was true. The move from Dimondale to Ionia had been rushed and, fourteen years later, there were still boxes in the garage that had never been unpacked. Some closets also had unexplored boxes and all storage areas needed to be cleaned and sorted. Running the Reformatory had been an all-consuming effort and I was ready to decompress with mindless housework. But not full time. I sought help and found Beata Zarebski, who came in twice a month to do most of the cleaning. As Bill had hoped, I took over cooking and enjoyed that immensely. Gardening continued to be summer therapy.

In August of 2001, Bill and I traveled to Philadelphia for the ACA conference and the NAAWS Warden of the Year Banquet. My mother came along, as did John and Katie. Many of my corrections friends shared the event, including Luella Burke and Sharon Johnson Rion. When the plaque was presented, John saluted me, wearing the DOC honor guard uniform. I had known he was a member of that unit. What I did not know was that he was wearing their new gear for the first time in public. A few of the old head wardens later told me that they were brought to tears by the tribute. Pictures show Edna wiping away tears, also. I felt the Warden of the Year honor was as much for the Reformatory staff as for me, just as the honorary doctorates had been, but enjoyed the evening, nevertheless.

One of the reasons I retired the first day I was eligible was to spend more time with Bill. We had enjoyed trips to Thailand, Canada, Mexico, and throughout the US while I was working, but wanted to travel more extensively and without the demands of work always in the background. After ACA, we drove west through the Canadian provinces to Vancouver and Victoria, BC. We squeezed in a visit in Corvallis with Tina, Brad, and niece Johannah before heading to Bill's brother's home in the Los Angeles area. While there, we heard the news of the Sept. 11 attacks and watched with horror as the scenes from the Twin Towers and Pentagon played endlessly and the news of the heroic diversion and downing of another plane was revealed. Visits with family in San Diego and Houston were more precious than ever that year.

As promised, Mason Thomas arrived in January 2002. John's wife, Kris, was working outside the home two days a week and I was recruited to watch Mason during the morning and early afternoon. Because Kris's hours were quite early and travel from Ionia to Lansing in the winter was uncertain, I would stay overnight before and during my two-day stint. On the first afternoon, I often took Mason to visit my mother, heading home to Ionia the afternoon of the second day. This continued for Mason's first nine months and helped create a wonderful bond between us. Reading stories, singing, dancing, and especially the arrival of the garbage truck were highlights. When a second pregnancy was announced, my services were again solicited. I am guessing John and Kris hoped to save child-care expenses for Mason as well as the new little one, but I nixed that. I wanted the same quality experience with this new baby, who turned out to be Trevor John. Kris's schedule was the same, and Trevor and I had a great time exploring the outdoors since he was a June baby. The garbage truck arrival continued to be a hit. As with Mason, my babysitting ended when Trevor reached nine months, but regular grandson visits with Edna continued until she passed.

I have often wished I had not been working when the Kime grandchildren were born. We visited after each birth and usually made an annual trip to San Diego. On a few occasions, the Kime family visited Michigan; however, I know relationships with Mason and Trevor are different from what I have with Keeler, Lychelle, and Mandalyn. Health concerns informed Christopher's decision to live in San Diego, but time and distance are enemies of grandparent bonds.

Although I had many offers to be a consultant, the only one I accepted for pay was with the Moss Group. I had known Andie Moss through the ACA Women's Task Force and respected her integrity. She asked if I would work for her to develop a training video for implementation of a federal law, the Prison Rape Elimination Act, also known as PREA. Since the filming was going to be in Idaho, she suggested I might also visit and evaluate the situation at a prison with a challenging culture in Washington state. Her firm had contracts through NIC for both projects. I enjoyed the work and still occasionally will have someone comment that they had seen me on the PREA video. Unpaid consulting was for the Michigan DOC. Pat Caruso was the new director, and she expanded leadership training that had been initiated by Bill Martin. The new training, Women's Leadership, was initially delivered by NIC trainers with Luella and me observing. The model was then adopted by Michigan's Training Division. As a result, Luella and I had multiple opportunities to help deliver the three-day sessions. While room and board were provided, we happily donated our time for this excellent effort. I also delivered training about cognitive work when asked.

I retired from the Independent Bank board when I retired from the Reformatory, but added board responsibilities for Ionia County Memorial Hospital and the Ionia District Library. Rotary, BPW, and the Chamber Ambassadors continued to be interests, and I decided literacy tutoring with adults a couple days a week would also be interesting. The nice thing about volunteer activities is that you can vacation when you want to—and I did. Bill and I traveled to England, Scotland, and Wales as well as the Maritime provinces in Canada. We continued to explore the USA together.

I also took trips with gal pals Luella Burke and Sharon Johnson Rion, usually to conferences. One year we combined an AWEC conference trip with a stay on Ocracoke, a barrier island off North Carolina. Luella and I developed a presentation for a WWICJJ conference that we called To Be or Not to Be... One of the Boys. This was a lighthearted presentation that started with Luella dressed in a very feminine manner and me in a mannish suit with a floppy bow tie. I would usually enter from the rear of the room with a cigar in one hand and a brandy glass in the other, shouting, "Party, party, where is the party?" We would then describe highlights of our careers, adding and subtracting accessories as the talk progressed, ending with us wearing similar business garb. The message was that there is no absolute right way to get through a career, but being true to your own values will be healthiest. We thought this would be a one-time performance, but we ended up doing it on multiple occasions. Sadly, the difficulties women were experiencing in the male-dominated world of corrections continued to need amplification and discussion.

Conferences for ACA, NAAWS, WWICJJ, and the Association of Women Executives in Corrections (AWEC) were held in interesting cities around the country, and I attended to enjoy traveling and staying in touch with friends in the business. The AWEC was formed about the time I retired, an outgrowth of NIC training for women holding leadership positions that Susan Hunter had fostered. I recall arguing for the inclusion of wardens as executives as the group discussed membership categories. Luella later followed Sharon as the executive director of that group; my contribution was to serve as treasurer one year.

It was at an AWEC conference that six of us bid on a silent auction item—a week at a villa in Spain. Bill's health was not good, and he had told me he did not expect to be able to travel to Europe, but that I should go if I got the chance. When the bids were reviewed, ours won the villa. I came home from that conference excited about my news. Bill, on the other hand, clouded up. I did not understand why he was not happy for me. He explained he was feeling better, and he had always wanted to go to Spain. Well, I wanted to travel with him, too, so we planned a trip that involved Bill and me visiting Madrid with side trips to smaller cities, followed by a time when the AWEC friends would join us. Bill would then fly home. As it turned out only four of the original six were able to make the trip. Luella, Marilyn Chandler Ford, Lurline Baker Kent, and I would rent a van, drive to the villa for our week there, and stay in Madrid for a few days before returning to the USA.

That turned out to be a memorable trip. Lurline's medication bag was stolen at the airport. I was supposed to be watching the luggage and was mortified that I fell for a scam. One person asked for help and while I was responding, the person with her snatched the bag. I did not even know Lurline had been ripped off until she returned and started looking for a pill. Some of the missing meds were urgently needed, so our first order of business when we got to the villa in Pego was to find a doctor. But first we had to find the villa. Luella was driving the van, which had a manual transmission. Pego was an old city and we got lost in an area with very narrow streets. Finally, after a lot of lurching around, something blew and we were immobilized, blocking the street. Fortunately, Marilyn knew a little Spanish and had a badge. When the police came, she was able to get their help to contact the rental company. Unlike in the USA, no replacement vehicle was forthcoming. Instead, they sent a tow truck and promised a taxi. The tow truck driver was loading our van when we realized he was about to take off with all our luggage. We managed to get our possessions out of the vehicle and were stuck on the side of the street. The locals were kind, though. They gave us fruit and water and let us use their restrooms. A young man finally turned up to take us to the villa. We provided the address and squeezed into his cab. By now it was dark. We spent a long time driving around resort developments, but none seemed to be the one we wanted. Finally, our driver asked a dog-walker if he knew the location of our address. It turned out we had been on the wrong mountain. With good directions, we finally found the place that would be home for the next week.

The villa was lovely, with a view, a pool, and an outdoor kitchen. Previous visitors had compiled information about local services, including English-speaking doctors. We noted the phone number and location of a couple of promising ones. The next morning, our driver returned, and we headed to a major city for a new van. Then we went looking for a doctor. The woman we found not only replaced Lurline's drugs (at a cost less than her USA co-pays), but also recommended a great place for lunch and good shopping sites. We had a great time on the White Coast. Our villa was not on the ocean, but did catch cool breezes in the evening.

On our last day, we visited Pego again, leaving the van at a shopping center far away from the narrow center streets. Luella was shopping for a dress for her fortieth wedding anniversary. She had tucked the van's "key" into her bra. This was an oblong plastic piece necessary to unlock and start the van. After shopping for a while, we went for lunch. In Spain, a siesta period is observed after lunchtime until around 4:00 p.m. When we finished our lunch, we headed for the van, but discovered the key was missing. Luella decided she had left it in a dressing room in one of the shops. We returned to the shop—closed for siesta. We returned to the restaurant. They were closed for service, but the people cleaning up took pity on us and provided water and sangria. They also knew the proprietor of the shop and called her for us, but she would not return until after siesta. That was a relief because a holiday was coming up and some shops would not be reopening at all. We had to no choice but to wait. During that time, though, we toured a local church we would not have otherwise seen, so we got a little culture along with the delay. We were sorry to leave Pego, but we had a good time in Madrid before winging our way home.

On March 20, 2008, I was again with gal pals, this time Tekla and Luella. We were touring Carol Howes's prison in Coldwater to see her dog training program when I was summoned to the warden's office for a phone call. My mother had been in an auto accident, and I was urged to get to Lansing's Sparrow Hospital as soon as possible. As it turned out, she had suffered a stroke or heart attack while driving to a hair appointment and her car had drifted off the road into a cornfield. We had a Quaker-style service in her home later that month. Mason composed a song about her that celebrated her kindness and tea-making; we sang it at Chere and Mike's home the evening before and again the day of her service. She gave unconditional love to her family and was a wonderful role model.

Kristy and I were trustees for the estate and, since I had time, I got to wrap up the trust. It is a tribute to the way we were raised that there was no friction as assets were distributed. Kristy wanted the family home where she grew up; Tina and I wanted the farmland in Indiana, and Chere was happy with funds. After the sisters had made their selections of possessions, grandchildren had a chance to choose items significant to them. It was a warm and wonderful process. Tina and I call our farm Withrow Acres; it abuts the farmland Charles's sister, Barbara, left her children. They call their part KT Acres; it was farmed as one parcel by a cousin, Ron Gamble, until he retired, and then we leased it to his cousin.

»»»»»»»»»»»

In the winter of 2014, we had a wonderful gift. Lychelle, our oldest granddaughter, decided to do her high school junior-year internship at the Chamber of Commerce in Ionia. Christopher accompanied her and they flew into Grand Rapids. January in Michigan can offer all kinds of weather. In their case, it was a blizzard. We made it to Ionia and stopped at the Meijer store for supplies they needed. The parking lot was as empty as I had ever seen it. Then we headed out of town. We made it most of the way up our drive, but the curve and hill defeated my trusty RAV4. I backed down and tried it a couple more times, but feared I would slide off into the trees, so got as far up as I could and told my passengers we would have to hoof it on in. Lychelle was prepared for Michigan weather and hauled out her Uggs, grabbed a suitcase, and headed for the house. Christopher had only tennis shoes and got wet and cold feet during his trek. The neighbor's dog made such a racket that the neighbor came out to see what was going on. Luckily, he got on his tractor and pulled the RAV4 the rest of the way up the drive.

Before Christopher returned home, he wanted to see John and his family, so we arranged to meet in St. Johns. By this time, we were experiencing a January thaw. Rain had turned the gravel drive into a skating rink, although paved roads were fine. We made it out and home with no problem, but I knew the curve and hill would again be treacherous, so backed the car into a neighbor's drive near the paved road and walked to the house. Chris had a plane to catch the next day, so this seemed to be the safest way to ensure we could get out. Morning came and we left the house, pulling Chris's luggage on a sled. Unfortunately, the car could not make the slight incline needed to get us back on the drive. One of my Ionia gal pals, Toni Buys, was retired; I turned to her for help. When I called, she was cleaning her basement. She switched gears and came to take us to the airport—an act for which Chris and I will be forever grateful.

Lychelle enjoyed her internship. She learned to drive on ice and in snow and experienced the rhythms of small-town life. The chamber's annual awards event was during her tenure, so she helped organize that. After she had gone home, I discovered that friends she had made in Ionia had taken her on a trip to Lake Michigan which had included adventuring onto an icy pier. Extremely dangerous, but she survived. She found the town quaint and local high school interesting. We missed her cheerful presence when she went home after six short weeks.

The remaining winter of 2014 turned out to be severe. On several occasions, I returned from shopping and was unable to make it up the hill to get home. After parking at the Martinez's place and carrying groceries over another neighbor's lawn the second or third time, I told Bill that if I fell and broke a hip, we would both have to go into a home. He promptly got on the internet and found a variety of condos in the Lansing area. I scoped them out, found one in the East End development that looked most promising, and called the realtor. After a tour, I was sold. Bill also found it acceptable. We had not sold our Ionia place when we put in the offer, but had the resources to close on our new East Lansing home. After we moved, I discovered we would pay property taxes to Meridian Township and school taxes to East Lansing, the two highest rates in the area. On the other hand, the new place had a basement big enough for the pool table Bill had always wanted, had lots of storage, was a stand-alone condo, and, best for me, allowed the owners to plant around the foundation. I had mourned giving up gardening and now could keep my hand in, but with limits to keep me from planting more than I could maintain.

Living near family and friends was a delight. Kristy got me involved in Planet Fitness and we worked out three times a week. Denise introduced me to her book club, and, to my delight, Jane White turned out to be one of the members. I could attend Mason and Trevor's school events and more conveniently stay with them when John and Kris traveled. The local library turned out to be a good one; however, I did not volunteer for literacy tutoring or Friends of the Library activities. Attending to Bill's health concerns had become a full-time job and volunteering was not possible, although I did squeeze in work with the Democrats to help elect President Obama to a second term.

»»»»»»»»»»»

In early 2016, I had a surprise! Ron Hammond, my journal partner from the Reformatory, had tracked me down in East Lansing and written a letter expressing thanks and gratitude for the opportunities he had received due to participation in the STP program. The US Supreme Court had just ruled that offenders who had been sentenced to life for crimes committed before they were eighteen should be reviewed with a goal of converting that sentence to a term of years. Hammond said,

> *Many times over the years I have wanted to throw in the towel, to give up all hope and succumb to the environment around me. But, each time I would hear your words and remember you telling me to always remember that views towards "Crime & Punishment" swing like a pendulum, constantly moving from one extreme to the other. That one day in my lifetime that pendulum may swing in my favor. Even though that force that controls that pendulum is out of my control, how I choose to live my life isn't. I could either continue to make positive changes, to strive to do what is right and maybe one day have a chance to go home, or I could*

give up, surrender to my environment and guarantee that I would never go home. I could squander any opportunity before it ever presented itself.

As I read the letter, I kept waiting for a request for support for his resentencing process. That did not come. Either Mr. Hammond was setting me up for a future request for help or he had a genuine desire to let me know how much he had appreciated the opportunities offered by the STP program. Time would reveal his actual motivation.

»»»»»»»»»»»»

The Network members remained friends. Tekla Miller moved to Durango, Colorado, after retirement and invited us and another friend, Adria Libolt, to visit. She had an active program planned: meeting her Durango girlfriends, traveling to Telluride and Silverton, a day exploring Durango, and a jeep ride up a mountain to enjoy the vistas. Denise Quarles had taken that trip on an earlier visit and assured us that the views were worth the ride, so we bundled up and headed out. The driver provided blankets for the open-air jeep. We were glad for those since it was a nippy morning. The road was initially asphalt, then good gravel, then a narrow, dirt two-track. It was twisty, with no guard rails to spoil the view. Snow began to appear along the roadside. Suddenly, we hit a bump and lost traction. The driver's foot was hard on the brake, but we were sliding backward toward a steep drop-off. Probably because we were all corrections-trained, no one screamed or even cried out. We finally came to a stop when the jeep backed into one of the few sturdy trees along that stretch. The driver suggested we get out while he attempted to get enough traction to extract the jeep. I was happy to comply. He got the jeep turned around and asked if we wanted to continue upward or go back. My recollection was that Tekla was the only one who favored going up. Adria, Denise, Luella, and I voted to retreat. Our driver seemed happy with that decision and found us a safe adventure on the return trip. A great lunch awaited us at the bottom of the mountain.

At home, Bill's health continued to deteriorate. He encouraged me to travel, and I did. Amtrak offered roomettes on the route to Portland, Oregon. Tina would pick me up there or in Albany, where she and Brad were living on a friend's farm. Then, I would travel south to Sacramento and home through the Colorado mountains, paralleling by rail the routes Bill and I had so often traveled. That trip was so much fun that Sharon Johnson Rion and Gladys Beckwith each joined me one time. Sharon and I spent three wonderful days at Powell's bookstore in Portland and enjoyed exploring the big city. That was followed by a visit with Tina and Brad and then home. Gladys met her daughter in Portland and toured Oregon beaches while I visited Tina and Brad before we headed south and then east. Chris, Katie, or our friend from Ionia, Beata Zarebski, would stay with Bill while I enjoyed my train jaunts.

When I returned from Durango, Bill confessed to heart palpitations and shortness of breath which had started just before I left. We went to the emergency room; he was admitted and had a stent installed in a heart artery. He had near constant back pain, relieved only when he stretched out on a couch or bed. His vision was failing, and he had to switch from reading to listening to books on CD. Luckily, after he had listened to everything I could find from the district and state libraries, he was able to use a free service from the Library of Congress. A player for a USB drive was provided and books could be downloaded to the drive. I believe every title he requested was available. That was a wonderful service. However, after another visit to the ER where he was told, brusquely, that he would just have to live with pain, he said he had had enough. With John's help, I was able to arrange for hospice at home. Christopher and Tina came to assist with Bill's care. John, his family, Chere, Kristy, and her son, Salem, were the support team. Bill passed the day before Katie's birthday, on December 2, 2018. He had lived eighty-seven remarkable years and shared thirty-five of them with me, so I felt quite lucky.

Bill had prompted me to consider the historical implications of my appointment as the first woman to run a facility for men in Michigan. After the awards and honors attendant to retirement, he pressed me to write a book about the experience—with him as editor. I promised to write but delayed starting because I did not want to tell him he could not edit my words. He had written his own autobiography and self-published it, so he should have been able to understand an author's desire to retain a personal voice; on the other hand, he had both written and edited during his work life and after retirement. He even confessed that he would almost rather edit than write. I was understandably reluctant to turn him loose on my words. So, after his death, I used writing to revisit my life and work, to heal, and to keep my promise to share my experiences in corrections.

As I was completing the first draft of this book, Mr. Hammond's attorney, Katherine Root, contacted me. She asked if I would testify on his behalf. My approach to prison work had always been compartmentalized. Judges sentenced and I imprisoned; I had never advocated for a prisoner's release. My reflexive response was to refuse; however, I also recalled my dismay at seeing young men arrive at the Reformatory looking at a life in prison after a senseless murder. I was also aware of the brain research that had influenced the Supreme Court's decision to direct review of sentences for juvenile lifers. Thus, I told Ms. Root that I would consider testifying, but wanted to meet with Mr. Hammond before making a final decision. She arranged a meeting at the Handlon Michigan Training Unit (MTU) in Ionia.

Ron Hammond was fifty-one when we met. He had transferred to a facility that housed younger offenders because he was part of a peer counseling program. While at MTU, he had become involved in college studies called the Calvin Prison Initiative. Enrolled students are housed together at the prison and given a laptop with access to the internet as well as free books and tuition leading to a bachelor's degree in faith and community leadership as a major and social work as a minor. Those serving life or long sentences are given priority for enrollment in the hope that they will positively influence prison culture. For the few who are released prior to completion of their degree, books, tuition, and housing are provided. Since the above major is available only to prisoners, most who are released elect to make their social work minor their major. Upon completion of the five-year program, assistance finding employment is offered.

For those who are unfamiliar with Calvin University, I should note that it is associated with the Christian Reformed Church. Certainly, their decision to invest in prisoners is a testimony to a belief that individuals can change. And change was what I believe I detected in Ron Hammond. He was quietly confident about his future. College had helped him mature and develop self-awareness. He said he had found a purpose for his life and, even if not resentenced, would be able to contribute to his community of prisoners. When Ms. Root and I left the prison, I told her I was ready to testify if necessary. As it turned out, the state appellate defenders' office was able to negotiate an agreement for resentencing Mr. Hammond to a term of forty to sixty years.

I went to the resentencing hearing and found it packed with family and friends of the victim. Even though Michigan's law regarding resentencing of juvenile lifers states that an agreement between the state appellate defender's office and the prosecutor binds the judge, Shiawassee County's jurist decided to hold a full hearing, with statements from the victim's family, the prosecutor, and Mr. Hammond. The judge tried to coerce the prosecutor to change his mind; fortunately for Mr. Hammond, the prosecutor stood fast. Finally, the judge reluctantly brought his gavel down, affirming the negotiated sentence and offering a possibility of parole for my former journal partner.

After the hearing, the prosecutor was escorted from the courthouse by armed deputies. I met briefly with Ms. Root and her coworker and Mr. Hammond's family. To my surprise, the family was not celebrating. The Ron Hammond they had seen off to prison had brought heartache to their mother and trouble to their lives. While they hoped he had changed, they were wary. I thought back to my initial response when asked to testify for him and realized we were all unlikely to believe people had changed until presented with proof. It will be interesting to see if Mr. Hammond gets the opportunity to provide it. To his credit, he sent me another letter thanking me for coming to his hearing.

He also said,

> *I truly owe you my life. Not only did you teach me how to take responsibility for my past, present and future, you also inspired me to find my true calling—service. The Calvin Prison Initiative is providing those of us in the program with a tremendous opportunity to serve, both in and out of prison. It is very exciting, but I would not be here now if it wasn't for you. I can never thank you enough for preparing me for this moment. Prison by design is an uncomfortable environment to live in, however, thanks to you, I have known true freedom and peace for a very long time. I have been free from anger, free from resentment and free from self-hate and more importantly, I have found true joy in helping others. To say you have been an inspiration would be an understatement...you have been a true role model in every sense of the word.*
>
> *Thank you.*

That letter was a wonderful affirmation of my belief in cognitive programming and provided an exclamation point for my years of corrections service. (In 2021, I learned that Mr. Hammond had been granted parole and was living in Grand Rapids and finishing his work at Calvin.)

At the end of February 2020, Tina flew to Costa Rica to meet me for a ten-day ecotour of that beautiful country. This was with a group of public radio listeners who cheerfully loaded onto a bus with a proud native who knew his homeland's flora and fauna. We saw butterflies and iguanas, hummingbirds and huge spiders, monkeys, sloths, and more. We explored cloud, rain, and arid forests, rode rafts and boats, and even saw the cloud forest from swinging bridges. Most days involved some hiking, but all included great food and conversation. The trip was enhanced because of sharing it with Tina, who is an easy companion. As we were heading for the airport, one of our fellow travelers confided that she had lost the close relationship she had shared with her sister, but that after seeing how much fun Tina and I were having, she was going to make an effort to rekindle that bond.

We had been insulated from the world's news while touring, but our last stop was at a Pacific Coast resort, and people began to hear about a new illness that was spreading around the globe. It was the time of COVID. My thrice-weekly workouts with Kristy were converted to long walks. The Zonta Club and book group meetings to which Denise had introduced me were conducted via Zoom. The planned trips to Washington state, Ireland, the Netherlands, Belgium, and Germany were put on hold, possibly never to be. We all put on masks, stayed home, and hoped for an end to the illness and death. Vaccines came along and I elected to be double vaxxed and boosted but continued to mask when going indoors. As Kristy and I walked her bassets through all kinds of weather, I became a convert to the pleasure of walking.

Luella had been diagnosed with liver cancer, but her surgeon gave a positive prognosis; sadly, he was wrong, and the cancer returned. She began chemo and she and Arnold planned her funeral. Then he began to exhibit symptoms that suggested a stroke. A friend took him to the ER and he was admitted; sadly, he also was diagnosed with cancer, both lung and brain; he passed on St. Patrick's Day 2021. I made several trips to Ludington and Grand Rapids to support Luella in the first six months of that year. Her chemo had been put on hold in February and she was physically improved by the time of Arnold's memorial service in June. Her son, Dennis, urged her to move to Nashville to live with him and his wife, Gwen. I was happy to be of help to Luella as she bravely packed the few items she would take and sorted and distributed a lifetime of memories before putting the home Arnold had built, and she had lovingly furnished, up for sale.

»»»»»»»»»»

June 2021 was when Keeler and Mandalyn would graduate from college and I was determined to participate in the limited festivities permitted. Katie also wanted to celebrate, so she bought a plane ticket to San Diego. After that, she planned to travel back to Michigan with me. She had never experienced a cross-country train trip, so I bought adjacent roomettes on Amtrak and planned a day in San Francisco on the route home. Since I was traveling west anyway, I decided to start in Oregon, with Tina and Brad. Soon after Arnold's memorial service, Mason dropped me at the East Lansing Amtrak station bound for Chicago. From there, it was off to Portland, then south to Albany for the first stop. Tina and Brad showed off their new (to them) home and all the gardens they'd added. I got to help Tina care for Henry in Eugene for a day. I had forgotten what a delight it was to operate on "toddler time." We strolled through a park, played with a water table, watched the ducks on the river, observed machinery depositing branches, played on slides at every possible point, and helped Johannah and Will prepare for his surgery (tendon repair following participation in a charity event). I had run out of knitting material and Tina provided beautiful yarn she had spun and dyed from which I made a wonderful earflap hat for myself. Brad and I had the traditional tasting of IPAs and we all enjoyed meals that included garden bounty. Artichokes were on the menu for most meals—what a treat!

From Albany, I traveled to Los Angeles for an overnight and change of trains and then on to San Diego, arrival scheduled for the eleventh of June, the day before Keeler's graduation. On that final leg of travel, I had a text from Chris inquiring whether I had heard from Katie. I had not. She had not deplaned from her scheduled flight. Keeler did some detective work and found Katie's friend Ebbie Stankowski, who was to have taken her to the airport. It turned out that Katie had waved off Ebbie, saying she was not feeling well and was going to drive herself to the hospital. Chris checked with the most likely hospital and was told Katie had been found unresponsive at home and was pronounced dead soon after she arrived. I was glad I was with the rest of the family by the time this sad news was given. We hugged and cried and had a family council and decided Katie would have wanted Keeler to have his big day (Mandalyn's graduation was to be virtual, so no travel to San Francisco for that) and we would go ahead with the celebration. The following day, Chris would fly to Houston, to be joined there by John, coming from Michigan. They would find a funeral home, arrange care for Katie's home, and deal with her many cats. I was glad those two had formed a bond that allowed them to support each other during that difficult trip. My job was to write Katie's obituary with input from the rest of the family.

I then had to cancel Katie's Alaska Airlines flight to San Francisco and Amtrak ticket back to Michigan. The former was almost comical. When the customer service rep told me I could get a refund (on a $79 ticket) if I paid a $100 cancellation fee, I responded that I could do math and that I did not think I would accept that offer. Amtrak was much better to deal with, refunding all tickets promptly. The overnight in San Francisco was made less painful when Karen Gibson, who had planned to act as tour guide for Katie and me, pivoted to the role of consoler and offered a lovely lunch at an outdoor restaurant on Treasure Island followed by an afternoon at her home in Oakland's hills, with birds flitting through the trees and lush greenery all around. I had dreaded the train ride home, with the adjacent empty roomette reminding me of Katie's absence. Instead, there was a pleasant surprise; a young couple next door was clearly enjoying their trip. As often happens, the train was late getting into Chicago's Union Station, but Amtrak provided a nice room along with a box dinner and vouchers for breakfast and lunch. Mason met me at the station, and I was reunited with Violet and Charley, the kittens I had adopted in late 2020.

»»»»»»»»»»»»»

Out of the meeting with Mr. Hammond described earlier came an opportunity to work with the state appellate defenders' office. This involved writing reports for possible resentencing of offenders who had committed serious crimes when they were under eighteen that resulted in life sentences with no possibility of parole. I have enjoyed reviewing files and creating reports. This project, while paid, is something I would do for free because the offenders were so young when they committed their usually senseless crimes. I understand the loss victims' families have experienced; however, locking someone up for life cannot restore the life of their loved one. Most advanced countries cap murder sentences at about twenty years, with the understanding that most offenders will no longer be a threat to society after that amount of time in prison. Few have capital punishment. Michigan, thank goodness, has never had it since becoming a state. I think a review of the cases of these young offenders is a good way to sort those who might be assets if released from those who still pose risks. The Supreme Court clearly intended most to be considered for resentencing to a term of years and eligibility for parole. So far, only one of the four cases for which I have written a report has had a hearing at which I had to testify.

»»»»»»»»»»»

In July, Luella turned eighty, and I joined other Michigan friends in celebrating that milestone with her in Nashville. We ate, shopped, laughed, talked, and ate some more. I got to be the chauffeur through the lovely winding roads near her adopted home. While enjoying BBQ, we even got some local Nashville sound. Sharon joined us for lunch at a place famous for the quality and quantity of their fare—especially the biscuits—and, other than overshooting the place when navigator Luella missed it initially, we had a great time. After days of celebrating, I flew from Nashville to Houston to help Chris continue the work he and John had started in preparing Katie's home for sale. We worked hard and had only a few tasks left when it was time for us to head home. Chris and Susie made a final visit in August to complete the work and find a realtor. With cleanout help from Ebbie and Butch Stankowski, the place sold promptly. Chris was executor of the estate and we discovered, to my dismay, that Katie's will specified that her father and I were to inherit. Fortunately, my Edward Jones broker introduced me to a legal term, disclaimer, and I was able to disclaim all inheritance and have it pass to Christopher, as was only right. He generously helped his children with college expenses. I think Katie would have liked the way we worked together to share the proceeds from her life.

In September, Luella came to Michigan for a visit with me and her Ludington friends. I collected her from the airport, and we had some quiet time at the condo and a meal with Denise before the whirlwind visit "up north" with her many good friends. One of these, Joan Nelson (a recent widow herself), offered us a room. I enjoyed getting to know this quiet, lovely woman. Like me, she is a reader and introduced me to a new author, Marie Benedict, who has written a series about women throughout history whose stories have not been told. While Luella was enjoying a morning of canasta, I made a beeline for the wonderful yarn shop Ludington boasts. Christmas gift ideas were given a start with beautiful yarns found there. Another stop was the artist collective housed in Luella's first Methodist church home. When a new church was built, the building became an arts center. There was a painting of a woman on a horse that was so evocative of Kristy that I couldn't resist getting that for her birthday. Denise met us for another chance to break bread together as we returned from Ludington. We ended Luella's Michigan visit with a stay at the Burnt Toast Inn in Ann Arbor. Of course, we had to pass through Brighton on the way, which gave us an opportunity to meet and eat with her Brighton friends.

Another unexpected death had me returning to Nashville in October. Sharon Johnson Rion's husband, Bill, experienced a fall in their home that led to his passing. Luella suggested I stay with her for a few days so we could travel together to the funeral. Sharon had family staying with her immediately after what was a wonderful celebration of Bill's life, but she agreed she would appreciate a few days visiting with me when family left. So, Luella and I had time together again, followed by a very sad and quiet time with Sharon. To boost my spirits, I routed myself through Indiana and suggested an impromptu breakfast with family there. Cousin Carol Royer offered to host, so I got to see other cousins: Ron Gamble, Judy Dykstra, Marilyn's daughter Miriam, and all their spouses. These cousins are descended from my mother's sisters and continue to form a close-knit clan.

Even with deaths, illness, and an ongoing pandemic, I am grateful to be entering the final chapter of my life in a pleasant location near family. Life is good.

Work is what you do, not who you are. If you can afford to retire young, go for it. I was fortunate to retire at fifty-two with a pension and good insurance. Because I am blessed with good health, I have been able to travel with family and friends, spend time with Bill and my mother as they aged, provide childcare for John and Kris, watch local grandsons develop into fine young men, celebrate distant grandchildren's college graduations, visit out-of-state relatives, and enjoy activities in my community. I continue to give back to corrections, but only in areas I am passionate about. Time with family and friends is always more enjoyable when there are no deadlines lurking or inboxes to clear. Retirement only consigns you to the refuse heap if you elect to go there.

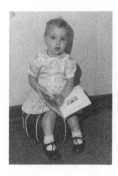

Pam, about age one, with a beloved book at her home in Romney, Indiana.

Pam, about age two, with her parents, Charles and Edna Withrow, Romney, Indiana.

In a dress she had made, Pam, age seventeen, in the 4-H Fair Queen Contest, Lafayette, Indiana (1966).

Grandparents Alma and Lewis Withrow in their home with son Charles and daughter Barbara Ronksley and their families on the farm in Romney, Indiana, at Thanksgiving. Left to right, seated: Tom Ronksley, Lewis, Alma, and Tina Withrow. Standing: Bob, Barb, Diana, Bob Jr., and Kay Ronksley; Chere, Pam, Kristy (baby), Edna, and Charles Withrow (1963).

Bill Kime, Pam, and Corrections Director Perry Johnson at a conference (late 1970s).

Ron Hammond in the STP yard at the Michigan Reformatory (late 1990s).

"The Network" on Tekla's boat: Tekla Miller, Denise Quarles, Luella Burke, and Pam (early 1980s).

Pam and Bill Kime at the Grand Valley State University honorary doctorate event (2000).

Pam receiving an honorary Doctor of Laws from President Lubbers at Grand Valley State University, Allendale, Michigan (2000).

Edna Withrow with Pam before presentation of honorary Doctor of Public Service from Ferris State University, Big Rapids, Michigan (2001).

Bill Kime, Luella Burke, Pam, John Cordell, Edna Withrow, and Sharon Johnson Rion at the North American Association of Wardens & Superintendents' Warden of the Year Presentation, Philadelphia (August 2001).

Pam at the entry drive of the Michigan Reformatory with a sign created by the facility's furniture factory workers which announced her selection as Warden of the Year by NAAWS (2001).

Edna Withrow's 80th birthday photo in the foyer of her home. From the left: Chere McCloskey, Pam, Tina Withrow-Robinson, Edna Withrow, and Kristy Withrow with Charles Withrow's christening gown in the background (2007).

Pam with Luella Burke starting "To Be or Not to Be...One of the Boys," a popular presentation at conferences after both were retired (early 2000s).

Pam with her sisters and their families at their first home in Haslett, Michigan. From the left: Pam; Sean, JP, and Karen McCloskey; Kris, John, and Mason Cordell (Trevor is elsewhere); Tina and Brad Withrow-Robinson; Salem Withrow (Kristy's son); Chere and Mike McCloskey; Lizzie, Sabrina, Mike Jr., and Max McCloskey; Trevor Cordell; Kristy Withrow; Matt, Sebastian, Zoe, Rebecca, and Madeleine McCloskey. Note: Johannah Withrow-Robinson and Bennie McCloskey, Matt and Rebecca's youngest son, are not pictured (2008).

Visiting the San Diego Kime family with son John and his family: Susie Kime, Trevor Cordell, Keeler Kime, Mason Cordell, Pam, Mandalyn Kime, Chris Kime, Lychelle Kime, Kris Cordell, and John Cordell (2012).

ACKNOWLEDGMENTS

Thanks to Mission Point Press, where I found warm support and competent assistance in the adventure of self-publishing. Thanks also to my initial editor, Sharon Johnson Rion, whose gentle guidance improved the first draft and who has joined the cadre of sister-friends who make life rich, and to Tanya Muzumdar, the final editor, who helped me finish this book. My husband, Bill Kime, insisted I write about the experience of being Michigan's first woman to head a male prison and encouraged me to retain the many documents which provided support to the narrative.

Thanks also to Corrections Director Perry Johnson, who determined that women belonged in Michigan corrections and took the risk of appointing me to be the first woman to head a camp for male felons and followed that by naming me superintendent at the Michigan Dunes. His successor, Robert Brown Jr., later appointed me warden of the Michigan Reformatory, the oldest prison in the Michigan system, making me the first woman to run one of Michigan's three penitentiaries. Both directors gave me freedom to implement programs and innovate without interference, a great gift in a bureaucracy.

Susan Hunter was a wonderful role model whose mantra on the merits of a diverse work force were prescient and true; they guided my staff selections. And, of course, gratitude to my other sister-friends, Luella Burke, Tekla Miller, and Denise Quarles, who propped me up during the Jackson years and continue to provide fun and companionship. Many early readers helped improve this book, especially newer friends in the No Name Book Club. You know who you are. Thank you.

My professional life was enriched by courses offered at the National Academy of Corrections, which is part of the National Institute of Corrections. In my opinion, both federal agencies are a great investment of taxpayer dollars. Organizations also improved my career experience—first, the Michigan Corrections Association, then the American Correctional Association, followed by the North American Association of Wardens and Superintendents, and finally, the Association of Women Executives in Corrections. All offered an opportunity to learn from peers as well as professionals in other aspects of corrections work.

Those who read this book will intuit that none of the warden accomplishments could have occurred without the sense of self engendered by Edna Withrow, a purveyor of unconditional love. One sister, Tina, helped raise John; and my parents, Charles and Edna Withrow, and other sisters, Chere and Kristy, provided support through the rocky periods of my life.

Finally, thanks to my son, John, with whom I grew up and who has apparently forgiven the acts and omissions of a young mother. He and his family as well as all the Kime crew have brought much joy throughout the years and been wonderfully supportive as I enter the final chapters of my life.

A BRIEF OVERVIEW OF THE MICHIGAN DEPARTMENT OF CORRECTIONS

When I joined the MDOC in 1976, it was headed by Perry Johnson, only the second director in the modern era of corrections in Michigan. That era followed a riot at the State Prison of Southern Michigan, known as Jackson. Prior to 1952, the MDOC had a director, parole board, and three wardens, each of whom ran his prison as a fiefdom, and was responsible for seeking funds from the legislature for the facility's operation. Parole and probation officers worked for their county and reported to a local court.

Jackson, Marquette, and the Reformatory were penitentiaries. Jackson housed most of Michigan's male felons; Marquette was for those with escape histories or who were unmanageable at Jackson; and the Reformatory was for younger prisoners who were thought to be redeemable through education and work. These prisons had farms that raised livestock, fruits, and vegetables for the use of inmates and staff—many of the latter were housed adjacent to the prison. Prisoners were sent, on a rental basis, to work at farms and for industries in the communities in which they were housed, which helped balance the facility's budget. Prisoner discipline was maintained by use of solitary confinement, the lash or bat, and forceful streams of water. In the 1940s, a Michigan senator was assassinated, allegedly with the cooperation of staff at Jackson, who were said to have released prisoners to commit that crime. The problems revealed by a post-riot commission investigating the operations at Jackson resulted in the reformation of corrections in Michigan.

Director Gus Harrison was known as an honorable citizen without any strong political leanings. He was selected to reorganize the agency and develop new standards and policies. He created bureaus to oversee various activities of the MDOC. These were prisons, field services, industries, administration, health care, and programs. Some of these names are self-explanatory—prisons, industries, and health care. Field services was responsible for probation, parole, community residential programs, and work pass programming. Administration handled personnel matters for all MDOC entities (except prisons, which had their own personnel offices), budget requests to the legislature, and fiscal and property management. Programs not only investigated possible programs for use by the MDOC, primarily at prisons, but also conducted research for the agency. While Director Harrison had established the bureau, his successor, Perry Johnson, made extensive use of it. Under his administration, the Program Bureau developed risk screening to assist the parole board in their decision-making and a classification system that was objective, using misconduct, sentence length, and criminal history as the basis for security level placements. A regional prison system was also created, but never fully implemented due to community resistance to placement of prisons in areas producing large numbers of offenders. Finally, program statements for new prisons and public hearings related to siting those facilities were responsibilities of the Program Bureau.

Both Directors Harrison and Johnson had long tenures, which produced stability and predictability, a bonus for both staff and prisoners. Gus Harrison began to hire Blacks in the agency and Perry Johnson decided to open work inside all male prisons to women. When Director Johnson stepped down to a deputy director's position in the mid-'80s and Robert Brown Jr. took the reins, it seemed that continuation of the current culture was assured. My recollection is that, in 1976, the MDOC had roughly twelve thousand prisoners housed at the old penitentiaries plus the Michigan Training Unit, Muskegon Correctional Facility, and the Camp Program—a group of twelve camps stretching from Pontiac in the Lower Peninsula to near the Wisconsin border in the Upper Peninsula. When overcrowding resulted in riots at the penitentiaries in 1981, the legislature permitted time cuts to create a pool of prisoners eligible for parole. That legislation successfully reduced the population. However, a prisoner paroled early committed murders which resulted in a new timekeeping system and a ballooning prisoner population.

By the time Brown took over, several prisons had been added, including the agency's first women's prison. Prior to building Ypsilanti's Huron Valley Women's Facility, female felons had been housed by the city of Detroit at the

Detroit House of Corrections. In addition to the new women's prison, Florence Crane Correctional Facility, a converted mental hospital near Coldwater, housed lower custody women.

There was new construction for male felons as well: Huron Valley Men's Facility, adjacent to the women's prison, Scott Regional Correctional Facility in Plymouth, and two temporary facilities—Ionia and Jackson, in their respective communities. Prisons for men also included the Kinross Correctional Facility at a converted Air Force base near Sault Ste. Marie; Riverside Correctional Facility in Ionia at a former mental health facility (this was also the site of the Riverside Reception Center); the Michigan Dunes Correctional Facility in a converted Catholic seminary near Saugatuck; Lakeland Correctional Facility in Coldwater—also a conversion from a mental health facility; Phoenix Correctional Facility in Plymouth at the former men's Detroit House of Corrections; and Western Wayne Correctional Facility—also at a prison acquired from Detroit. Cassidy Lake was a training center for unemployed youth when the MDOC acquired it and continued to serve youth—offenders sentenced to the MDOC. Later, it was converted into the Special Alternative to Incarceration Unit (SAI)—a fancy name for a boot camp. Even with all the construction and conversion of existing facilities, prisoners were being housed in dayrooms, bulkheads, and formerly unused spaces at the penitentiaries.

Program Bureau staff estimated that a new six-hundred-bed prison would need to be opened every ninety days to keep up with the influx of offenders. Some camps were expanded, one added, and one even became a prison (Ojibway). Pole barns were erected as temporary, low custody housing on sites selected for permanent prisons. When the new prisons were completed, these pole barns were still needed. In fact, what started out as cubes for four prisoners quickly became housing for six, and then eight. In a building boom, many multiple-security prisons and a few maximum-security prisons were added to bring the population to over fifty thousand and the number of prisons to more than forty.

The Level V prisons were Alger, Baraga, Ionia, Oaks, and Standish. In addition to Scott, regional facilities were Bellamy Creek, Carson City, Mid-Michigan (now Central Michigan), Chippewa, Earnest C. Brooks, G. Robert Cotton, Gus Harrison, Macomb, Mound, Ryan, Saginaw, St. Louis, and Thumb. Level I facilities were Newberry, a mental health conversion, and Cooper Street, formerly part of Jackson, now also housing the SAI. Charles Egler Reception and Guidance Center uses part of Jackson and includes the newer Duane Waters Hospital. The Woodland Center was established as a mental health facility, and the Detroit Detention Center operates under an interagency agreement with Detroit as a pre-arraignment center. Most of the temporary facilities (Adrian, Boyer Rd., Straits, Parr Highway, and Pine River) have been incorporated into the adjacent prisons. Hiawatha opened as a temporary facility and was absorbed by Kinross, which subsequently closed most of the original facility, leaving only 320 minimum-security beds at the former Kinross site.

Facilities that have closed include the Camp Program, Camp Branch, Camp Koehler, Cassidy Lake, Deerfields, Dunes, Florence Crane, Huron Valley Men's, Mound (now the Detroit Detention Center), Ojibway, Phoenix, Pugsley, Riverside, Ryan (later Detroit Re-Entry), Scott, Southern Michigan, and other parts of Jackson, Standish, Western Wayne, and West Shoreline.

Over time, parole officers became state employees as did probation staff. Community corrections centers were established for early release, disbanded, and then restored—as alternatives to parole revocation, places to deal with alcohol or drug issues, or housing for parolees without a supportive home placement.

When the modern MDOC was created, it was governed by a commission, which approved policy and selected the director, insulating the agency from politics. Unlike many state correctional agencies which changed heads whenever the governor changed, Michigan was spared that instability. Governor Blanchard abolished the commission, which, predictably, resulted in rapid changes in directors. Brown was replaced by Ken McGinnis from Illinois, who brought a completely different culture to the agency. He was succeeded by Bill Martin, who brought leadership training and left operations to seasoned professionals. When Martin left to head the Michigan Realtors, Bill Overton became the second Black director and served until Pat Caruso became the first woman to head the MDOC. She built on Martin's leadership training by adding sessions for women, and, most significantly, began a process of community engagement and prison programs that resulted in a decline in the prisoner population and the closing of some prisons. As a result, she was selected by her peers as the best director in the country and ironically, while celebrating this event, was advised she was being replaced, following the election of Governor Snyder. A county sheriff, Dan Heyns, was named director and, again, brought a culture unlike that established by Harrison, Johnson, Brown, and Caruso. After a difficult period, he was replaced by Heidi Washington, who has continued to oversee a declining prisoner population and who has supported a culture more akin to that of most of her predecessors than that of persons without experience in the MDOC.

As a personal aside, my son John decided to join the department without letting me know. When I found out he was interviewing to be an officer, I asked if he wanted me to put in a word. He refused, saying that if he could not get an officer's job without my help, he did not want it. He was a great officer, was promoted to sergeant, and then offered to the training division on a temporary basis. He never returned to prison duties. He continued in the training section, with a brief detour into public information, and currently leads the New Employee Training section.

PRISONS AND THEIR OPERATION IN MICHIGAN (1976-2001)

People without a background in corrections who read early versions of this book had many suggestions for expanding descriptions of operational details; however, I felt an appendix would be a better place for such information. This appendix tackles prison operations in categories, so readers can find descriptions if they have questions.

CUSTODY LEVELS:

When I started with the MDOC, there were five custody levels.

Minimum was for the twelve camps reporting to Camp Control, the dormitories or farms overseen by Marquette and the Michigan Reformatory, or the cellblock and farms adjacent to Jackson. This level was for offenders close to release with very good disciplinary records and no history of escape. Lifers were not permitted unless they had a release date from the parole board; homosexuals were excluded because most minimum-security units offered dormitory-style housing and because all had minimal staffing. Communal restrooms, showers, dayrooms, and dining were the norm. Access to recreation was at scheduled times and the yard was typically available during daylight hours if an offender was not at work or school. For example, Camp Brighton, which housed 140 prisoners, typically had a lieutenant and one officer on the 8:00-4:00 shift, a sergeant and two or three officers on the 4:00-12:00 shift, and a corporal and two officers on the night shift. The reason staffing could be so spare was that offenders were nearing release to corrections centers, or on parole and had the incentive of furloughs and work pass as well as visits with family in an outdoor picnic area (with families bringing in food on Sunday) during good weather. To keep these perks, most prisoners elected to follow the rules. Another reason staffing could be minimal was that most work needed to maintain operations was done by the offenders. Most minimum-security facilities had no fences, or, if fenced, there was no razor wire as a deterrent to escape; however, by 1987, fences with razor wire were the norm. Prisoners were assigned to work or school, and in the camps, most had assignments. Hobbycraft and other leisure time activities were encouraged. Camp operations were directed by a camp supervisor. Units associated with prisons had deputies or assistant deputies responsible for operations, depending on the number of offenders housed. Larger units might have a captain, lieutenant, and multiple sergeants to supervise activities.

Medium was for well-behaved prisoners with any sentence length who were not eligible for minimum. Most housing was in single cells, but prisoners had keys to their room or padlocks to secure their cells. Staff could override the prisoners' keys with what was termed "toplock," a disciplinary sanction. At Jackson, staff could use a master-locking system to prevent the unlocking of the cell doors if a prisoner was found guilty of misconduct. Showers, restrooms, dining, and dayrooms were communal, and staff scheduled when these were available and supervised showers. Recreation and yard times were also scheduled and supervised. Staff oversaw prisoners preparing food, doing laundry, and performing cleaning and maintenance tasks. Prisoners were assigned to work or school; however, some idleness was common due to the lack of assignments. Hobbycraft and other leisure time activities were encouraged. The size of groups on the yard was not usually regulated. Visiting rooms were welcoming and included a play area for children. The rules, however, limited contact to a kiss and embrace at the beginning and end of the visit, and to holding hands. Perimeter security was double fencing topped with razor wire and reinforced by an armed perimeter vehicle. An arsenal was stocked with rifles, shotguns, handguns, restraint equipment, and chemical agents. Each shift was supervised by a captain, two lieutenants, and several sergeants, and the prison itself had a warden, deputy warden, and two or three assistant deputies who managed custody, housing, and treatment areas. Treatment included the school, religious services, recreation, the library/law library, and hobbycraft. Also reporting to the warden were a business manager (who oversaw finance, food service, warehouse, and maintenance activities), a personnel officer, a records office supervisor, an administrative assistant, and a secretary. Health care staff reported to supervisors in Central Office. (In

1976, medium-security prisons were Muskegon, the Michigan Training Unit, and a portion of Jackson.)

Close was for prisoners beginning a sentence of life or term of more than six years, for escape risks, and for those who had failed in lower custody. Prisoners had a sink and toilet in their single cell and staff controlled the locking and unlocking of the cell door. Showers were communal, but scheduled and carefully supervised. In addition to the usual work and school assignments, prison industry work was offered. These jobs paid better than most other prison work and were highly valued by the prisoners. Yard groups were usually segregated by housing unit to limit size as well as to keep prisoners who might have conflicts separated. The number of prisoners permitted in indoor recreation areas was limited. Other aspects of management were similar to that of medium. In addition to Health Care staff, Industries staff also reported to Central Office supervisors. (In 1976, a portion of Jackson and the Michigan Reformatory offered close custody housing.)

Maximum was for very serious escape risks and offenders who presented a danger to staff or other prisoners. Like those in close custody, offenders had a sink and toilet in their cell. Fewer prisoners were permitted to shower at a time and staff closely monitored this activity. The number of prisoners permitted to eat, recreate, and gather for any reason was much smaller than in close custody. Other aspects of management were similar to that of medium. (In 1976, Marquette was the sole maximum-security prison.)

Within close- and maximum-security prisons, two more custody levels were used:

Administrative segregation is often described as the jail within a prison. Prisoners who committed acts of violence (or had materials for them) or attempted to escape were often sentenced to punitive detention. That is a sanction for misconduct that is usually followed by time in an administrative segregation unit to permit staff to observe the prisoners' behavior while carefully regulating access to weapons or victims. While in administrative segregation, prisoners are housed in a cell with a sink and toilet and permitted one hour of out-of-cell activity (typically outdoors) five days a week. They are fed in their cell, usually though a food slot in a solid door. They are secured by handcuffs attached to belly chains when out of cell. Some especially violent prisoners may also wear leg irons/chains. Restraints are removed when prisoners are secured in recreation or shower areas. Showers are generally permitted three times a week in a caged area. Cell lights may be controlled by staff, and cell furnishings are secured to the floor or wall and are often made of stainless steel. There is a single, small window in each cell. While in administrative segregation, offenders who need law library materials request these and they are delivered. General library services are made available. School materials are delivered and picked up. The chaplain makes rounds. Visits are non-contact.

Protective segregation is the other custody level. Offenders often request this status because they fear sexual assault or retaliation as a result of events in the community. Sometimes they have borrowed money in prison or gambled and lost and cannot pay debts and request protection. Occasionally, staff initiate placement in protection when they become aware of a situation that will place a prisoner in danger. The federal prison system is usually willing to accept law enforcement or corrections staff who are convicted in state courts, as it is believed these individuals would be in danger if housed in our prisons.

»»»»»»»»»»»»»»

When the massive prison expansion began in the late '80s, custody levels were adjusted to accommodate the new housing configurations that ensued. New levels were determined to be I, II, III, IV, and V (and briefly, VI, when Michigan flirted with the super-max craze). Level I corresponded with minimum. Level II incorporated most elements of minimum, but had a secure perimeter like medium, and permitted well-behaved lifers and other prisoners with long sentences to be housed in low custody. Cubes (enclosed areas with head-high panels, but no door) in pole barns housed four-to-six (later, eight) prisoners, and rooms at Kinross housed three men, while the Dunes had dorms, rooms with multiples, and single rooms. Level III corresponded with medium; however, crowding in the system caused single rooms to be converted to doubles. Level IV and close custody were similar, and Level V and maximum corresponded. Part of the reason for the failure of the super-max (level VI) concept, in my opinion, was that it was in Ionia. For most prisoners, being in Marquette in Level V was less desirable than being downstate in Level VI. Marquette has the oldest cells in the system (except for the Reformatory's G Block) and the long, cold winters there are tough for people who have grown up below the bridge, which is the case for most Michigan prisoners.

MDOC PRISONER POPULATION

In 1976, there were around twelve thousand prisoners in the system and female felons were still housed by the city of Detroit at the Detroit House of Corrections. By the time I left in 2001, the population was nearing fifty thousand. (Note that it exceeded that for a time, but has been dramatically reduced since I retired; in 2021, it housed around thirty-five thousand.)

TERMINOLOGY:

Commissary or prisoner store: An operation that permits prisoners to purchase food and supplies not provided by the prison. In 1976, the store was operated by staff and purchases were made with scrip (coupons representing money from the prisoner's account), which were exchanged for items. Subsequently, tokens replaced scrip, with the predictable problems of gambling and extortion. Later, when computerization made it possible, orders were filled by staff with funds taken directly from prisoners' accounts. Privatization of store operations is now in place.

Gas: A chemical agent applied under pressure. Often referred to as tear gas. Current active ingredient is a derivative from hot peppers; hence the term "pepper spray" is sometimes used.

WHY DO COGNITIVE WORK WITH OFFENDERS?

In a little more than twenty years, the field of corrections came full circle on the issue of programming for offenders. Until the 1970s, most professionals in the field at least paid lip service to the notion that their primary aim was the rehabilitation of those sentenced to their care. Then a scholar named Robert Martinson concluded—or more accurately, was widely claimed to have concluded—that so far as rehabilitation programs are concerned, "nothing works." While corrections agencies kept most of their education programs, which some studies showed as having value, many other treatment programs were dropped or curtailed, and prisons came largely to be regarded as human warehouses. But, over time, the recognition grew that separation of the prisoner from the public was not an adequate goal, since most prisoners would be out in a few years, and that releasing an educated, but still criminally oriented, person does the community no favor.

So, in the 1990s many correctional agencies returned to the belief that there is a responsibility to try to help prisoners change for the better. Many understood that this involved much more than teaching or preaching. Criminal behavior would not be abandoned so long as criminal patterns of thinking and viewing the world were retained. To this end, some in the field adopted a variety of cognitive programs which offered offenders an opportunity to change the way they think, with the goal of changing how they behave. These cognitive programs were usually divided into two types—cognitive skills training and cognitive restructuring. To describe the former somewhat simplistically, it operates from the premise that learning social skills—apologizing, negotiating, or introducing oneself, for example—will cause the offender to change his thought processes related to interpersonal relations. Social-skills training will result in a change from criminal thinking to pro-social thinking. (The premise of all cognitive work is that thinking drives behavior, so change in thinking will result in behavioral change.)

Cognitive restructuring, however, is the effort with which I am most familiar, and the one selected for use at the Michigan Reformatory, where I was the warden for fifteen years. It was chosen because the facility housed young adult prisoners, most of whom were first-timers, and it was thought that a change effort would be most likely to be effective with individuals relatively early in their criminal careers. We initiated this program for two reasons: first, prisoners wanted something which would help them avoid future criminal behavior (they phrased this as wanting "programs, not warehousing"), and second, I thought such a program might help staff see themselves as having a role beyond merely keeping the lid on, addressing the problem of burnout.

Let us look first at the prisoners' issue: In Michigan, as in many other states, newly arrived prisoners go through a reception process where their deficiencies are identified, and programs are recommended to address these needs. Academic and vocational training programs are often prescribed, as are therapies to address substance abuse or mental health problems. Most facilities also offer recreational and religious programming, and some include music or other arts and crafts.

So, a prison sentence may include a complete blueprint for self-improvement. The problem, though, is that unless the thought processes which drive criminality are addressed, prisoners prepare to leave facilities as well-educated, healthy, religious, work-ready crooks. Parole boards are then faced with the dilemma of telling offenders, who have completed all the reception-prescribed efforts, that they will not be paroled because they still present a risk to the public—a risk which exists because the attitudes and beliefs which permitted the prisoner to rape, rob, or kill are still operating. These thinking processes, while they do present some danger to prison workers, usually are not harmful in the closely managed prison environment; but in the community, an unchanged parolee will often commit new crimes rather quickly.

As for the program's benefits for staff, these were twofold: first, staff used the techniques for change in improving their own lives. Self-reports indicated cognitive processes were used to stop smoking, improve interpersonal communication in a marriage, lose weight, and change exercise patterns. Secondly, the program can indeed be effective in reducing staff burnout. I have frequently observed a phase which occurs about five to seven years into the careers of those who have elected to remain corrections officers: the employee becomes sour, depressed, cynical, and often either hostile or apathetic. This comes, I think, from the recognition that he or she is facing twenty or more years of dealing with offenders who have many of the same characteristics as immature adolescents. What had seemed to be a promising career now looks more like a sentence. But since the hours, pay, and benefits are good, the employee elects to plod on with minimal job satisfaction. Involvement in a cognitive restructuring program can provide some such employees with new meaning in prison work. In a few cases, it may spark return to college and a renewed interest in promotional opportunities. At a minimum, it offers variety in what is otherwise a rather routine shift.

So, these are some of the things a cognitive restructuring program can do, but what exactly is a cognitive restructuring program? As initially practiced at the Michigan Reformatory, it involved three phases, and all prisoner participants and most staff facilitators volunteered to take part. The program (termed STP, an acronym for Strategies for Thinking Productively) was introduced by explaining the concepts basic to the cognitive approach: thinking controls behavior; all people have attitudes and beliefs (which differ for different people); and repetitive thoughts become automatic cycles. It was further explained that changing thinking requires auditing thoughts, and that change is hard work which cannot be imposed by others. Prisoners must want to change, must choose to change, and must put forth individual effort to make initial changes and then continue their efforts over time to ensure these changes become part of a new approach to life.

The program depended heavily on the concepts of criminal thinking developed by Yokelson and Samenow in their three-volume work, *The Criminal Personality*. One of the first steps was to give prisoners a list of thirty-six criminal-thinking errors developed by these authors, and to ask them for their own thoughts about the list. It is interesting that invariably most of the discussion which ensued did not have to do with whether the thinking errors were properly described, but rather with whether they are in fact criminal. After all, from an offender's point of view, everybody thinks like that. A few of the most common, and most dangerous, thinking errors are listed below:

Victim stance: When the criminal is held accountable for his irresponsible actions, he blames others and portrays himself as a victim. If the world does not give him what he thinks he is entitled to, he views himself as poorly treated and, thus, a victim.

Energy: The criminal is extremely energetic. His high level of mental activity is directed to a flow of ideas as to what would make life more interesting and exciting.

Anger: Anger is a basic part of the criminal's way of life. He responds angrily to anything he interprets as opposing what he wants for himself. Anger is, for the criminal, a major way of controlling people and situations.

Pride: Criminal pride is an extremely high evaluation of oneself. It is the idea that one is better than others, even when this is clearly not the case. Criminal pride preserves his rigid self-image as a powerful, totally self-determining person.

Failure to consider injury to others: The criminal's life involves extensive injury to those around him. However, he does not view himself as injuring others. When held accountable, he regards himself as the injured party.

Ownership: When a criminal wants something that belongs to someone else, it is as good as his. "Belonging" is established in his mind, in the sense that he feels perfectly justified in getting his way. The criminal considers himself a decent person with the right to do whatever suits his purposes, and he views the world as his oyster. He views people as pawns or checkers, waiting to be dealt with as he wishes. This thinking is habitual and without malice.

If these errors are considered in a little more detail, most people who have worked with offenders will readily recognize how well they apply:

Victim stance is an element in almost every criminal's thinking. Offenders explain their decision to commit crime by blaming others: They were with a bad crowd. They only had the gun to scare the store owner; if he had not fought back, he'd be alive today. The little girl wanted his affection. All these rationalizations take place even though the crime description indicated that the perpetrator was the leader, that he had discussed how he'd kill "the dude" if he resisted, and that the molested child screamed and cried. The egocentric view of the perpetrator as the victim permits him to avoid responsibility for his actions. One of the first tasks of STP was to get the offender to see that portraying himself as a victim is a major block to change—that it is actually a weakness. The position of strength is to accept responsibility for his actions. A victim cannot control his fate.

Those who work with offenders often remark that although these men are poorly educated, they clearly have adequate mental processes. This is reflected in the energy the criminal expends toward things he wants to do or make happen. While in confinement, many prisoners quickly complete their GED studies because the stimulation level is so low in prison that school is one of the most interesting activities available.

Anger is, for many prisoners, an emotion to be substituted for all other feelings. We actually had had to develop a "feelings" list because many men in prison had no label for their feelings other than anger—they were angry when sad, lonely, hurt, or ashamed.

Some of the crimes which lead to juveniles being waived to adult prisons result from pride. The typical case I saw involved a youth at a party. He was "disrespected," went home and got a gun, and returned. He displayed the weapon, other guns came out, someone ended up dead, and I had a new prisoner, often for life with no possibility of parole. If the same prideful attitude continued in prison, this young man would be involved in frequent fights and would spend a significant amount of time in segregation. He demanded respect from staff; they responded that he would get respect when he had done something to earn it. (It is easy to see the conflicting beliefs operating in this transaction!) This offender was often ready for cognitive restructuring because he was experiencing significant losses as a consequence of his behavior.

One of the most notable characteristics of offenders is failure to consider injury to others. If, in a robbery, a weapon was present but not fired, the prisoner says, "Nobody got hurt." The fact that there was a dollar loss to the robbery victim, not to mention the terror and loss of trust experienced by the person at whom the gun was pointed, was ignored. If physical injury did not occur, the prisoner viewed this as no harm. The loss of relationships with family and friends due to criminal activity was also discounted by offenders. One young man I worked with did not understand why his mother and sister were the only family members who visited him after his conviction for sexually assaulting a friend's child. That his family might suffer as a result of the offenders' actions was rarely considered.

Ownership, the error that permits criminals to take others' property simply because they desire it, often creates problems in the prison environment, where such activity can incur the death penalty. One prisoner at the State Prison of Southern Michigan stabbed another to death because the former had stolen and sold the latter's coat (for $4). When the thief refused to return either the money or the coat, he died. While this is an institutional example, think of all the news reports of kids being killed for shoes and jackets. What may be hard for us to grasp is that the killers are not acting out of malice—they simply want what someone else has and they will have it, with or without the victim's acquiescence. Their faulty thinking permits them to do something they would otherwise agree is wrong: taking the life of another.

Returning to the process of the program itself, during Phase I some tools, called "thinking reports" and "journals," were introduced. Prisoners practiced using them, and barriers to change were discussed. This first phase involved fourteen lessons usually presented during sixteen sessions over eight weeks. (The series of lessons can be accelerated; but reducing the frequency would lessen the excitement of self-discovery and was not recommended.) Not surprisingly, many prisoners had never considered that they have control over their behavior. They used phrases like, "I went out"; "I caught a case"; or "I had to shoot him," as if their criminal behavior was reflexive and completely unplanned, and, in some cases, unsought. There was a real excitement as offenders discovered that they do have control over their lives and that they do not have to continue to live in the constant grip of anger, fear, and hostility.

For those interested in more detail, let me mention that the lessons in Phase I, and the structure for Phases II and III, are contained in the *Options* manual available through the Information Center at the National Academy of Corrections. This manual was originally developed for a naval correctional facility (under a grant from the National Institute of Corrections) by Dr. Jack Bush and Brian Billodeau.

Naturally, those wishing to deliver this program will tailor it to their own circumstances. At the Michigan Reformatory, for example, we decided to focus primarily on offenders with violent backgrounds. While Phase I was open to all prisoners and replaced traditional group counseling, volunteers serving for crimes of violence had priority in Phase II.

In Phase II, up to forty prisoners participated in five groups, with each group meeting three times a week. Phase I groups were closed, and while they started with about ten members, they often ended with only four or five. Phase II groups were open, adding members as individuals dropped out, went to segregation, or transferred from the facility. We determined that groups no larger than eight were most productive, with six or seven seeming to function best. Also, Phase II participants lived together in a small (seventy-eight-bed) housing unit within the nearly one-thousand-bed close-custody portion of the prison.

Each group started with a check-in, which permitted the facilitators (always two; a case manager and an officer were the desired team) to take the temperature of the group. Sometimes the group members rated themselves from one to ten, with "one" representing little interest and energy, and "ten" indicating wild interest and enthusiasm. This was intended to be a quick way for participants, including facilitators, to transition from other prison activities and to convey their readiness to begin the session.

The work of the group was to listen to a thinking report presented by a member and to ask the member questions designed to help him understand the thinking which supported the behavior described in the report. The entire one-and-a-half-hour session was devoted to a single thinking report. Following the session, the facilitators documented and evaluated participation of the group members as well as that of the presenter.

A thinking report is structured as follows:

- A brief description of a specific incident where the prisoner got into trouble (or could have if caught).

- A listing of all the thoughts associated with this event. Prisoners are often prompted to "run a tape" of the event in their mind to recall specific thoughts.

- A listing of the feelings associated with the event. This sometimes prompts additional thoughts or permits participants to frame questions if there seem to be no thoughts related to a particular emotion.

- A sentence describing the attitude supporting thinking or behavior during the event. Sometimes there are multiple sentences.

- A sentence stating a belief supporting the thinking or behavior during the event. This often includes "should" or "ought" terminology.

- Sometimes, physical responses are also listed. As with emotions, recalling these responses may trigger additional thoughts or suggest ideas to others for useful questions to ask the presenter.

Each participant took a turn being the presenter, so there was some reciprocal value to being active; also, because some thinking errors are so common, participants may come to recognize their own errors while pressing another to clarify his thinking. Ultimately, prisoners selected target behaviors they wanted to change and presented thinking reports related to that behavior. Patterns, or cycles, of thinking could then be identified (earlier by other participants than by the presenter, ordinarily) leading to the design of interventions to prevent the cycle from reaching completion.

Once target behaviors were identified, prisoners were asked to journal daily during the remainder of Phase II. Journal reports were similar to thinking reports in structure, but they focused on efforts to change thinking in selected areas. The change effort may include thought stopping (cutting off or redirecting thinking) or bringing in thoughts about how the target behavior will harm loved ones or lead to sanctions, and may even involve replacing old attitudes and beliefs with new ones. Each prisoner was assigned a journal partner who reviewed the journal with him each week and helped him continue the process of identifying cycles and evaluating interventions. The journal partner would also help design journal projects which focused on changing attitudes and beliefs.

Journals were a way prisoners could track the success or failure of various strategies. They also provided staff with a measure of the participant's willingness to produce a sustained, focused effort. When the prisoner felt he had some level of control over a targeted behavior, journaling permitted him to move on and address another behavior.

Each quarter, a treatment team was held for each Phase II participant. During this session, the facilitators, the journal partner, and an officer working the housing unit talked with the prisoner about their perceptions of his progress (or lack thereof) in addressing target behaviors—those behaviors the prisoner had said he wanted to change. Sometimes lack of effort was so clear that the prisoner was asked to leave the program; if he then claimed he wanted to stay, a brief probationary period was offered, during which he would be monitored for performance on identified objectives. Occasionally, a prisoner would be so deficient in the ability to monitor his own thinking, or to present this to the group, that he would be terminated. However, literacy was not a requirement: many participants were low-functioning or involved in special education efforts, yet their ability to communicate their thoughts was unimpaired.

When participants entered Phase II, they were given the format for a relapse prevention plan. They worked on this throughout Phase II, and before moving to Phase III, had to present a thinking report to the group about the offense which brought them to prison, and a completed relapse prevention plan directed toward the criminal behavior. Most participants were involved in Phase II for nearly two years before moving to Phase III.

If the correctional system is willing to parole or let prisoners go to community residential placement upon the completion of Phase II, Phase III can be a community-based activity. This was not an option for Reformatory prisoners, many of whom were serving life or long indeterminate sentences; Phase III was conducted at the facility, but outside of the supportive Phase II unit. This part of the program continued the journaling effort and offered weekly group meetings which focused on participants' change efforts. Unlike the thinking report groups in Phase II, these were more interactive sessions, with members offering encouragement and support as participants continued to struggle with the difficult task of self-change. I also added a social skills element called the Warden's Dinner. While the food served was from the prison kitchen, we used serving bowls and platters; plates, glasses, and silverware; and even place mats and cloth napkins. Food was passed and conversation encouraged. Up to ten participants could be included and, since we never had that many Phase III prisoners, staff usually attended, even those who did not support the program. After dinner, the prisoners did the dishes and I counted silverware and other items. Since Phase III involved demonstrating pro-social behavior in a prison environment, participants were doubly challenged.

How do you start a cognitive intervention program if you should want to do so? As an example, I will describe our process. The effort at the Reformatory began in 1992, when four staff traveled to the National Academy of Corrections in Longmont, Colorado, to receive NIC-sponsored cognitive strategies training. We sent a counselor, a unit manager, a psychologist, and a warden, and returned with the intention of conducting cognitive skills training. However, through discussion and debate, we decided that the needs of the Reformatory population would be best addressed with cognitive restructuring. NIC came to our assistance again, with a 1993 grant which brought Dr. John (Jack) Bush and a Vermont practitioner, Brian Billodeau, to Michigan to train Michigan DOC staff, primarily those working at the Reformatory.

Following this, selected Reformatory staff traveled to Vermont to study the Violent Offender Program in operation there. Finally, in August 1993, the Reformatory's first Phase I group was started. Initially, most of the facility's eleven case managers delivered Phase I groups. As prisoners' initial interest was satisfied, we found that offering two or three Phase I groups regularly would provide sufficient replacement members for Phase II, and that this number was all that was needed to keep the waiting list short. Word-of-mouth advertising continued to be strong, however, as sign-up sheets were filled quickly whenever new groups were formed.

By the end of 1993, the first Phase II group had started meeting. Due to renovations, the space needed to house these participants as a cohort was still being used for segregation, however, so the residential phase did not begin until June 1994. At that time there were five Phase II groups with eight prisoners in each. Staff resources were becoming stretched as we experienced the growing pains associated with starting a new program.

At about the same time we started Phase II, it became apparent that we needed additional trained staff, so the original staff participants decided to train others in Phase I delivery. As time passed and word got out, employees in other Michigan correctional facilities, as well as individuals from other jurisdictions, expressed interest in this training, which we provided twice a year. We tried to limit these sessions to fifty or fewer, since this is hands-on training and we wanted to have enough trained facilitators to permit participants to leave the session with confidence that they could deliver Phase I. This training was usually delivered in Ionia, but when a facility in Michigan's Upper Peninsula decided to start a program, we took trainers to their site. In June 1997, the eighth semiannual training session was conducted. These continued until I retired in 2001.

To help staff improve their ability to test offenders' readiness for Phase III, we contracted (in cooperation with the Michigan Corrections Association) with the Geese Theatre Company from New Hampshire to demonstrate how drama therapy can be applied to cognitive work. It may be of interest, also, that corrections officers decided to try a Phase I group for segregated prisoners. That involved creating belly chains with extended cuff chains to permit charting for the group, and adjusting possession limits to permit chart paper and markers in segregation cells. Prisoners readily agreed to participate in this group, limited to five offenders. Although tried only once, these staff and prisoners demonstrated that groups could be conducted in segregation.

Finally, does the program really work? Kenneth L. McGinnis, the director of the Michigan Department of Corrections when the program was fully implemented, challenged us to show that participation resulted either in reduced misconduct within the prison, or in reduced recidivism as demonstrated by fewer parolees returning with new felony sentences. Grand Valley State University accepted the charge to provide research. Although I did not think that participation in Phase I alone would result in behavioral change, the researchers, led by Dr. Agnes Baro, elected to include a look at this possibility.

Dr. Baro's research findings (comparing Phase I and II participants to those in other voluntary self-help programs) showed a statistically significant decrease in Phase I participants' misconduct rates, when measured by length of segregation stay and in the number of disobeying a direct order (DDO) charges—the most common misconduct throughout the Michigan DOC. In Phase II, the reduction of DDO misconduct continued along with a reduction in assault misconduct. Since the agency automatically added a week to the release dates of offenders found guilty of misconduct in a given month, expansion of this program department-wide could provide a saving in the cost of housing prisoners. And since high-security beds are more expensive, any reduction in segregation stays also has a financial benefit. As far as I know, no research has been done on whether parolees who have gone through the program committed fewer crimes as a result.

So, with all this good news, is there a downside? Of course. Prisons operate best when there are routines. Change is viewed with suspicion. Anything which appears to be for the benefit of prisoners, and which requires additional effort from staff, will get close scrutiny and is likely to see some resistance. The

Reformatory is the oldest prison in the system, and staff attitudes sometimes reflected that history. "It's just another program." "You're coddling convicts." Or, "It may work for staff, but prisoners won't be able to use it" ("too dumb, too rigid, too steeped in the criminal subculture"). And participating staff were accused of being in bed with the administration. Then, too, since the STP unit was in the oldest part of the prison, and the cells were smaller than those elsewhere, a small dayroom with a microwave oven and color TV were created as some compensation, and a private yard with a vegetable garden was developed in a former outdoor exercise area. Even though most staff agreed that personal change is one of the hardest tasks any individual can undertake, there was still grumbling about these "perks" for Phase II prisoners.

These were just a few of the obstacles we faced. The case managers who delivered much of the program were entry-level professionals who were constantly being promoted, leaving shortages in these positions. Workloads increased with these shortages, so cognitive group work competed with the demands of other required activities. Physical plant issues also had to be addressed—a lack of group meeting rooms, for example. And scheduling was a problem. Since prisoner participants worked and went to school mostly during the day when staff facilitators were also most available, arrangements for release from assignments had to be made.

With these negatives, why did we keep offering STP? Because of the payoff: We saw both staff and prisoners grow and change in a positive direction due to their involvement in this effort. Of the original four staff who went to Colorado to learn about cognitive work, I was the only one who remained at the facility (and I had already reached my career goal); the rest were promoted or moved to a desired location. Of staff working in the program when I retired in 2001, one achieved her master's degree, and two officers pursued bachelor's degrees. (One completed his and was promoted to a central office position approving grants for programming department-wide.) Additionally, a very active participant was promoted at the facility, and others were promoted elsewhere. One even credited the program for leading to a move to a supervisory position in the Florida DOC—our loss and their gain. Many officers were finding their work more rewarding and looked forward to coming to work, rather than dreading it. Staff members who once were terrified of public speaking talked to large groups about STP with only mild butterflies. So many staff commented during training sessions that this information should be available to students that two employees formed a company to promote cognitive work in the schools to forestall the development of a next generation of criminals.

And we saw definite improvement among some of the prisoner participants— in one man, for example, who had such well-developed cheek muscles from clenching his teeth that he looked like he had marbles at the corners of his mouth, and who had rarely gone for a six-month period without a segregation stay. This man used STP to get a handle on his anger and was able to qualify for reduced custody. And we saw improvement in the one who convinced the parole board he had changed and finally made parole.

With some, the change may have been less complete, but may yet have impact in the future: For example, a prisoner who manipulated everyone all the time was finally able to see this and know when he was doing it, even though the manipulation eventually forced a move from the prison. And the one who started to get a clear look at himself and bailed out of the program was also clearly impacted.

We told all the participants, "You have three choices: change (with the potential to live a positive and productive life—even if that life is in prison), stay the same (with all the consequences you've experienced so far), or die." Those are the only choices, and they are the same choices all humans have. And really, the impetus for offender change was that their experience of prison, what was happening right now, was painful to endure and part of a cycle they could only escape by changing.

Vermont's Violent Offender Program research showed that cognitive restructuring is an effective change mechanism both in prison and when paroled. The positive STP research led to implementation of a NIC program offered at no cost, called "Thinking for a Change." That program included the cognitive restructuring of STP and supported it with skill- and problem-solving training. Because offenders need to know they have the option of personal change and that the tools for it are available, the Michigan Department of Corrections expanded this program throughout the agency. In addition to basic security, staff have the opportunity to help offenders grow out of criminal thinking and behavior. Since almost all prisoners eventually return to the community, I know of no better way in which we in corrections can contribute to our basic responsibility for public protection.

A CHRONOLOGY OF PAM WITHROW'S LIFE

Organizations

While in the Program Bureau:

Michigan Corrections Association

While at Camp Brighton:

added the American Correctional Association

While at the Dunes:

added the North American Association of Wardens and Superintendents, Allegan Co. NOW and Holland's Professional Women's Network

While at the Reformatory:

'86: BPW; '87: Rotary (Denise and I were inducted as the first women in Ionia's Rotary club. Charles came to that event.); '90: Domestic Violence Advisory Board; '92: MWSA Docent; '92: Ionia County 20/20; '93: Chamber Ambassador; Mar. '94: Ionia Women's Festival; May '94: Women Police of Michigan; '95: Ionia County Economic Alliance; '98: Association of Women Executives in Corrections

In retirement:

Zonta Club of the Michigan Capitol Area, after the move to East Lansing

Early Years

Summer 1966: Other Ongoing Employment

- Pollinating corn, Romney, IN

1970s: Other Ongoing Employment

- Two stints as a long-distance telephone operator, Bell Telephone, Lansing

College: Other Ongoing Employment

- Waitress in a bowling bar, fast-food cashier

Personal and Professional Events

1961: Maternal grandfather, Arza Macy, passed

1966: Moved to Michigan

1967: Graduated from Haslett High School

1968: Married Clint Cordell

1973: Graduated from Lansing Community College with a general associate's degree

1976

Michigan Department of Corrections (MDOC) Positions

Jun. 1976–Apr. 1977:

- Prison Counselor, Corrections Camp Program, Grass Lake

Personal and Professional Events

- Married the bus driver; separated 1982

1977

Michigan Department of Corrections (MDOC) Positions

Jun. 1976–Apr. 1977:

- Prison Counselor, Corrections Camp Program, Grass Lake

Apr. 1977–May 1978:

- Program Analyst, Program Bureau, Central Office

1978

Michigan Department of Corrections (MDOC) Positions

Apr. 1977–May 1978:
- Program Analyst, Program Bureau, Central Office

May 1978–Jun. 1981:
- Supervisor, Camp Brighton, Pinckney

Personal and Professional Events
- Paternal grandfather, Lewis Withrow, passed

1979

Michigan Department of Corrections (MDOC) Positions

May 1978–Jun. 1981:
- Supervisor, Camp Brighton, Pinckney

Personal and Professional Events
- Maternal grandmother, Lenora (Andrews) Macy, passed

1980

Michigan Department of Corrections (MDOC) Positions

May 1978–Jun. 1981:
- Supervisor, Camp Brighton, Pinckney

Boards
- Michigan Corrections Association

Speeches/Presentations/Articles

Oct.   Women in Criminal Justice panel for MSU's National Institute on Police and Community Relations

Oct.   Howell Kiwanis

1981

Michigan Department of Corrections (MDOC) Positions

May 1978–Jun. 1981:
- Supervisor, Camp Brighton, Pinckney

- Warden's Administrative Assistant, State Prison of Southern Michigan, Jackson

Oct. 1981–Feb. 1983:

- Assistant Deputy Warden, Housing, State Prison of Southern Michigan, Jackson

Boards

- Michigan Correctional Association

Out-of-State Training Attended

Mar. Workshop on Prison Discipline, American Institute of Justice, University of Toledo Law School

---

1982

Michigan Department of Corrections (MDOC) Positions

Oct. 1981–Feb. 1983:

- Assistant Deputy Warden, Housing, State Prison of Southern Michigan, Jackson

Boards

- Michigan Correctional Association

Conferences

Aug. Toronto American Correctional Association (ACA) w/Luella, Denise, and Tekla by train; Lu and me in cheap university housing; Denise and Tekla in the nice conference hotel; had a great time nevertheless

Out-of-State Training Attended

Nov. National Institute of Corrections (NIC) Boulder, two-week leadership training

---

1983

Michigan Department of Corrections (MDOC) Positions

Oct. 1981–Feb. 1983:

- Assistant Deputy Warden, Housing, State Prison of Southern Michigan, Jackson

Feb. 1983–Jul. 1986:

- Superintendent, Michigan Dunes Correctional Facility, Holland

Boards

- Michigan Correctional Association

Honors

1983–84: Superintendent of the Year, Michigan Jaycees Institutional Chapters

Conferences

May West Central Wardens and Superintendents conference in St. Paul w/Foltz, Handlon, and Wells (Perry Johnson's version of warden immersion training)

Aug. ACA Chicago with Bill

Oct. Michigan Corrections Association (MCA), Amway Hotel, Grand Rapids

Speeches/Presentations/Articles

Dec. Michigan State University (MSU) winter commencement speaker

May Women Police of Michigan (WPM)

Travels

May Toronto with Bill before the wardens' meeting in Traverse City

Jun. John and I traveled to visit Grandmother Withrow in Erie, PA, and then Chere and Mike in New Jersey. John then flew to Fort Lauderdale to visit Clint, and I took lobsters home for a Father's Day feast.

Aug. Canoe camping in Canada with Bill

Dec. Corvallis for Tina and Brad's wedding, then to the coast for a frigid stay with the newlyweds and the Robinson family; Chere and Kristy returned home, and Charles, Edna, John, and I went to San Francisco.

Personal and Professional Events

Jul. Charles's heart valve surgery at Cleveland Clinic

Feb. Official start date at the Dunes

Aug. Pam's hysterectomy

1984

Michigan Department of Corrections (MDOC) Positions

Feb. 1983–Jul. 1986:

- Superintendent, Michigan Dunes Correctional Facility, Holland

Boards

- Michigan Corrections Association

Honors

1983–84: Superintendent of the Year, Michigan Jaycees Institutional Chapters

1984: Holland Jaycees Young Woman of the Year

Conferences

Jun. Association of State Correctional Administrators (ASCA) meeting for Perry Johnson. Luella and I arranged much of this, Gary and Kay Wells hosted at their home, too.

Aug. ACA

Oct. MCA

Speeches/Presentations/Articles

Sept. Accountant's Club, Zeeland, "Correctional Facility Management"

Oct. Quota Club, Grand Rapids

Oct. Holland High School, "A Close-Up Look at Michigan's Prison System"

Out-of-State Training Attended

Feb. NIC Boulder, four-week "Managing the Internal/External Environment" (first meeting with Sharon Johnson; Luella Burke was there, too)

Travels

Jun. New Jersey for Father's Day with Chere and Mike, Charles and Edna

----

1985

Michigan Department of Corrections (MDOC) Positions

Feb. 1983–Jul. 1986:

- Superintendent, Michigan Dunes Correctional Facility, Holland

Boards

- Michigan Corrections Association

Conferences

Jun. MCA mini conference, Marquette

Aug. ACA NYC

Oct. MCA

Speeches/Presentations/Articles

Feb. MDOC public relations panel presentation in Bay City and Grand Rapids

Mar. Western Michigan University (WMU) criminal justice class, Dr. Bob Braithwaite

Apr. Kellogg Community College criminal justice class for Pete Drougalis

---

1986

Michigan Department of Corrections (MDOC) Positions

Feb. 1983–Jul. 1986:

- Superintendent, Michigan Dunes Correctional Facility, Holland

Jul. 1986-Jul. 2001:

- Warden, Michigan Reformatory, Ionia

1986–1987: Other Ongoing Employment

- Instructor, Montcalm Community College

Conferences

Jan. MCA mini

Mar. MCA mini

May National Organization for Women (NOW) state conference, Oakland University

Jun. MCA mini, Madonna College, Livonia

Aug. ACA Las Vegas

Sept. MCA (I was on the conference committee.)

Oct. North American Association of Wardens and Superintendents (NAAWS), Kentucky

Speeches/Presentations/Articles

Feb. Brighton Kiwanis

Apr. WMU class, "Correctional Institutions"

May MSU, Perry Johnson's class

Nov. Lansing Regional Chamber of Commerce

Out-of-State Training Attended

Jan. ACA training, Philadelphia

Sept. NIC Boulder, disturbance control training, one week

Travels

Mar. March for Women's Lives, Washington, DC

Mar. Las Vegas

Personal and Professional Events

May   40th-anniversary party for Charles and Edna

Jun.   John's high school graduation

Jul.   University of Michigan parent orientation

Jul.   Moved possessions to Bill's basement

Jul.   Official start date, Michigan Reformatory

Aug.   Married Bill Kime in the old deputy's house where I had an apartment for the first year at the Reformatory. He visited on Wednesday nights and I went to Dimondale on the weekends. Denise and Al hosted a reception at their home that evening.

Aug.   Hot-air balloon ride with Charles

Aug.   John to the University of Michigan

1987

Michigan Department of Corrections (MDOC) Positions

Jul. 1986–Jul. 2001:

- Warden, Michigan Reformatory, Ionia

1986–1987: Other Ongoing Employment

- Instructor, Montcalm Community College

Boards

1987-2001: Lansing Community College Advisory

Conferences

Jan.   ACA Atlanta. Filled in for Bob Brown; bunked with Luella and Sharon; Sharon slept in bathtub to get away from my high-decibel snoring.

Speeches/Presentations/Articles

Aug.   Lansing Community College graduation speaker

Out-of-State Training Attended

Apr.   Wharton Leadership training, one week, Philadelphia

Travels

Feb.   Skiing in the Soo with LeCureux plus other corrections friends

Personal and Professional Events

Sept. Prisoner Jordan escaped over the wall after hiding in the furniture factory for several days, beginning Sept. 9. He broke both ankles, so did not get far. I got points with staff for refusing to call the initial hiding out an escape; it frustrated the heck out of Director Bob Brown, though.

1988

Michigan Department of Corrections (MDOC) Positions

Jul. 1986–Jul. 2001:

- Warden, Michigan Reformatory, Ionia

Boards

1987-2001:   Lansing Community College Advisory

1988-2001:   Montcalm Community College Advisory

Consulting

Sept.   Presenter with Wharton School in Denver for leadership training (dinner at a lovely downtown B&B; mugged while strolling in my red silk dress, enjoying a cigar; beat the mugger with it)

Conferences

Aug.   ACA Denver

Oct.   MCA Shanty Creek

Speeches/Presentations/Articles

May   Grand Rapids Lions Club

Travels

Feb.   Skiing in the Soo with LeCureux plus other corrections friends

Dec.   Florida to visit with Charles and Edna in Lakeland

Personal and Professional Events

May   Geese Theatre visit

Sept.   Dinner with Gwen Andrew and Ruth Koehler. Gwen was Bill's boss when he worked for Mental Health and recommended him for his first MDOC job.

1989

Michigan Department of Corrections (MDOC) Positions

Jul. 1986–Jul. 2001:

- Warden, Michigan Reformatory, Ionia

Boards

1987-2001:   Lansing Community College Advisory

1988-2001:   Montcalm Community College Advisory

1989-1990:   Ionia/Montcalm Domestic Violence Advisory

Consulting

- Presenter, "Cross Gender Supervision," a one-day seminar for National Institution of Corrections (NIC)/North American Association of Wardens and Superintendents (NAAWS)
- NIC project to develop a competency profile for wardens and superintendents

Conferences

Jan.   NAAWS San Antonio, Menger Hotel

Jan.   ACA San Antonio

Feb.   Women Working in Corrections and Juvenile Justice (WWICJJ), Portland, OR

May   MCA mini, Jackson

May   MCA mini, Sault Ste. Marie

Aug.   ACA Baltimore

Oct.   MCA Detroit

Speeches/Presentations/Articles

Mar.   Montcalm Community College (MCC) Career Day

May   Michigan Corrections Association (MCA) Jackson, panel on ethics

May   MSU class for Perry Johnson

May   Holt Kiwanis

May   Michigan Youth Corps, Ionia, discussed corrections as a career

Aug.   MCC, "How to Deal with Prisoners"

Oct.   Ionia High School, "What is it Like to Be a Warden?" Mindy Stephens invited me; she is now a warden herself.

Nov.   Ionia Community Education, "Overview of Corrections"

Nov.   Ionia High School, "Career Development"

Dec.   Portland, MI Kiwanis

Out-of-State Training Attended

Aug.   NIC Boulder

Travels

Feb. Skiing in the Soo with LeCureux plus other corrections friends

Personal and Professional Events

Mar. Bill retired

Sept. Closed on Ionia home

Oct. Attended first Michigan Women's Hall of Fame Dinner

1990

Michigan Department of Corrections (MDOC) Positions

Jul. 1986–Jul. 2001:

- Warden, Michigan Reformatory, Ionia

Boards

1987-2001: Lansing Community College Advisory

1988-2001: Montcalm Community College Advisory

1989-1990: Ionia/Montcalm Domestic Violence Advisory

Consulting

May NIC advisory board meeting in San Francisco, CA

Jun. Sex Equity Conference, Greencastle, IN

Honors

- Women Police of Michigan certificate of recognition for outstanding service to the criminal justice field

Conferences

Jan. ACA Nashville

May MCA mini, Sault Ste. Marie

May Women Police of Michigan (WPM)

Aug. ACA San Diego

Speeches/Presentations/Articles

Feb. Luella and I braved a blizzard to present at Kinross re: "Women Networking."

Mar. MCC, 8th graders, career planning

Apr. Women's Resource Center, Ionia

Apr.	Cedar Springs High School
Aug.	ACA, "What is a Warden?" panel
Sept.	Lansing Jaycees, "What Is Prison providing for Tax $$?"
Nov.	WION (Ionia radio) interview
Nov.	Owosso Kiwanis
Dec.	WOAP (Owosso radio) interview

Out-of-State Training Attended

Nov.	Warden Peer Interaction, Los Angeles, CA

Travels

Feb.	Skiing in the Soo with LeCureux plus other corrections friends
May	San Diego and San Francisco

Personal and Professional Events

May	Bill's fishing buddies and spouses for dinner at our place
Jun.	Luella and Arnold's 25th-anniversary party
Sept.	Chaired Ionia BPW 70th-anniversary party

1991

Michigan Department of Corrections (MDOC) Positions

Jul. 1986–Jul. 2001:

- Warden, Michigan Reformatory, Ionia

Boards

1987-2001:	Lansing Community College Advisory
1988-2001:	Montcalm Community College Advisory

Conferences

Jan.	ACA Louisville
Aug.	ACA
Dec.	Grand Rapids Sentencing Options

Speeches/Presentations/Articles

Mar.	Speaker for Lansing Community College (LCC) Corrections Institute graduation
Mar.	Lansing Business and Professional Women (BPW), "Non-Traditional Roles for Women"

May	MSU, Perry Johnson's class
May	Cedar Springs High School
Oct.	Ionia Middle School Junior Achievement Class (ongoing for several weeks)
Nov.	Lakewood High School career day
Dec.	Calvin College
Dec.	Ionia High School, career options

Travels

Sept.	San Diego
Nov.	Baltimore for ACA nominating committee meeting

Personal and Professional Events

- Paternal grandmother, Alma (Caywood) Withrow, passed

Aug.	Israeli guests toured RMI
Sept.	Chris and Susie marry

1992

Michigan Department of Corrections (MDOC) Positions

Jul. 1986–Jul. 2001:

- Warden, Michigan Reformatory, Ionia

Boards

1987-2001:	Lansing Community College Advisory
1988-2001:	Montcalm Community College Advisory
1992-2001:	Michigan Women's Studies Association Friends

Consulting

Mar.	National Academy of Corrections (NAC), newly appointed wardens' training

Conferences

Jan.	ACA Portland, OR
Jan.	ACA Miami
Apr.	Michigan Women's Studies Association (MWSA), Grand Rapids

Speeches/Presentations/Articles

- Corrections Today, "Workplace Reality: Women Staff Tell It Like It Is"

Jan.	ACA, NAAWS-sponsored session, "Preparedness for Emergencies" with Art Leonardo
Mar.	Lansing BPW, "Non-Traditional Role for a Woman"
Apr.	MSU, Perry Johnson's class
May	Central Montcalm Middle School
Dec.	Lakewood Alternative Ed.

Out-of-State Training Attended

| Nov. | National Academy of Corrections (NAC), "Cognitive Approaches to Changing Inmate Behavior" |

Travels

| Sept. | Baltimore for NAC training |

Personal and Professional Events

Jul.	Reformatory passed accreditation audit, 100% mandatory, 98.6% non-mandatory
Jul.	Attended 25th Southwestern reunion, Indiana High School, where I attended through my junior year
Oct.	Charles passed.
Feb.	Party for Wells, Foltz, Handlon, Johnson, Brown, and spouses at our home

----

1993

Michigan Department of Corrections (MDOC) Positions

Jul. 1986–Jul. 2001:

- Warden, Michigan Reformatory, Ionia

Boards

1987-2001:	Lansing Community College Advisory
1988-2001:	Montcalm Community College Advisory
1992-2001:	Michigan Women's Studies Association Friends
1993-2001:	Independent Bank

Consulting

| Dec. | NAC planning for cognitive seminar, Longmont, CO |

Honors

- Michigan Corrections Association (MCA) Personal Recognition Award

Conferences

Oct.   MCA Romulus

Mar.   MCA mini (Geese Theatre presented)

Apr.   WWICJJ, Pittsburgh

May   Business and Professional Women (BPW) State Board

Aug.   ACA Cincinnati

Speeches/Presentations/Articles

Mar.   MSU, Perry Johnson's class

Mar.   Lakewood High School

Jul.   House of Commons, Lansing

Sept. MSU, Perry Johnson's class

Oct.   State Bar of Michigan, Grand Rapids

Nov.   Belding BPW

Nov.   Lakewood High School

Travels

Feb.   Skiing in the Soo with LeCureux plus other corrections friends

Summer Met up with Russ and Jo in Dubois, WY. We had a cabin on
a creek, and they came in their camper. Bill and I also visited the
Tetons, Eastern OR, Idaho, Montana, S. Dakota, and Colorado.

Personal and Professional Events

May   Wardens' meeting at MSU

May   Cognitive skills meeting

Jun.   Cognitive thinking reports training

Jul.   Abe French expressed interest in cognitive programs.

Jul.   Initial cognitive training session by Dr. Jack Bush and Brian Billodeau

Aug.   First cognitive steering-committee meeting

Sept. Clifford Lake Inn lunch w/ Mary Foy, Maureen Burns, Pat Heinrich
(Domestic Violence Board friends)

Oct.   Hall of Fame dinner Grand Rapids: I was the presenter for Cathryn
Hill Campbell, the first woman to head a facility for women offenders
in Michigan, Women's DeHoCo, which she helped design.

Dec.   Met with Agnes Baro (GVSU) to plan STP research

Dec.   First mention of STP Phase II

1994

Michigan Department of Corrections (MDOC) Positions

Jul. 1986–Jul. 2001:

- Warden, Michigan Reformatory, Ionia

Boards

1987-2001:   Lansing Community College Advisory

1988-2001:   Montcalm Community College Advisory

1992-2001:   Michigan Women's Studies Association Friends

1993-2001:   Independent Bank

Consulting

Mar.   Newly appointed wardens' training

Mar.   Presenter at a cognitive seminar for NAC, Longmont, CO

Speeches/Presentations/Articles

- Corrections Today, "Cognitive Restructuring—An Approach for Dealing with Violent Inmates"

Jan.   Calvin College

Feb.   Stanton Alternative Ed.

Mar.   MSU, Perry Johnson's class

Mar.   Cooley Law School

Apr.   Lakewood High School

May   Lakewood High School

Aug.   Six Lakes Alternative Ed.

Travels

Jan.   Florida to visit with Charles and Edna in Lakeland

Sept.   W/Bill at Vacationland Resort in the far western UP

Sept.   San Diego for ten days to meet Keeler

Personal and Professional Events

Jan.   DC Talk video filmed at the Reformatory; visited by NBC Nightly News w/Brian Williams

Feb.   Judy Putnam Booth news

Mar.   First three-day STP training conducted by RMI staff

Apr.   First mention of Luella/Bill Tiger bet. This was an annual ritual with the loser buying the winner and their spouse dinner. Bill generally won.

Apr.	Family gathering for Easter in Ionia
May	Met with Dr. Baro
Jun.	Three-day STP training conducted by RMI staff
Jul.	Met with Dr. Baro
Jul.	Keeler born
Jul.	Audit for reaccreditation
Oct.	Met with Dr. Baro
Nov.	Contact with Saul Hewish re: Geese Theatre's (John Bergman's, also) assistance with cognitive work
Nov.	Family Thanksgiving in Ionia
Dec.	A prisoner who had initially been my journal partner and later switched to a mail-room employee confessed he had plans to harm his current journal partner. He was commended, written misconduct reports, and then moved to another facility.
Dec.	Network Christmas in Ionia

1995

Michigan Department of Corrections (MDOC) Positions
Jul. 1986–Jul. 2001:

- Warden, Michigan Reformatory, Ionia

Boards

1987-2001:	Lansing Community College Advisory
1988-2001:	Montcalm Community College Advisory
1992-2001:	Michigan Women's Studies Association Friends
1993-2001:	Independent Bank

Consulting

- NY State DOC, "The Warden's Role in Guiding Change"
- NIC training strategies for "Success for Women Who Are Wardens," Cincinnati, OH

Honors

1995	Ionia Chamber of Commerce Athena Award
1995	Ionia Business and Professional Women's (BPW) Woman of the Year Award
1995-1996	Michigan BPW Woman of Achievement Award

Conferences

- WPM: Presenter, "Disastrous Relationships in a Correctional Setting"; panelist for "The Glass Ceiling"

Speeches/Presentations/Articles

- Panelist for "Leadership Culture" session at the WWICJJ Pittsburgh
- Panelist for MDOC probation staff training about the juvenile waiver process

Feb. East Lansing High School

Apr. Lakewood High School

Apr. Ionia Alternative Ed.

May Newaygo Alternative Ed.

Jun. Two sessions for the Appellate Attorneys' Association: Ann Arbor, "A Day in the Life of a Typical Prisoner" and "Dealing with the Corrections Bureaucracy When Visiting and Phoning Prisoners"

Dec. Lakewood Alternative Ed.

Travels

Mar. San Diego

Aug. New York

Oct. Thailand, gone four weeks

Personal and Professional Events

Jan. Three-day STP training conducted by RMI staff

Mar. Geese Theatre at RMI to train in role playing for prisoners in cognitive programs

Jun. Three-day STP training conducted by RMI staff in the Upper Peninsula

Jul. ACA reaccreditation visit

Dec. Three-day STP training conducted by RMI staff (noted 1996 desk and pocket calendars missing)

Dec. Chris, Susie, and Keeler visit. Keeler fascinated by the "dat" (cat) and not impressed with snow.

95-96: Completed a court-ordered project to provide legal aid for educationally disadvantaged and impaired prisoners

1996

Michigan Department of Corrections (MDOC) Positions

Jul. 1986–Jul. 2001:

- Warden, Michigan Reformatory, Ionia

Boards

1987-2001:	Lansing Community College Advisory
1988-2001:	Montcalm Community College Advisory
1992-2001:	Michigan Women's Studies Association Friends
1993-2001:	Independent Bank

Honors

1995-1996   Michigan BPW Woman of Achievement Award

- Women in Criminal Justice Hall of Honor Award

Conferences

Jan.   ACA

Aug.   ACA

Oct.   WWICJJ, Grand Rapids, cochair with Luella Burke

Speeches/Presentations/Articles

- ACA panelist, "The Benefits of Membership in Professional Organizations"

Jan.   Michigan State University Career Fair

Apr.   Portland Middle School

Oct.   Saranac High School

Nov.   Ionia High School

Travels

Mar.   Houston, Albuquerque, San Diego, LA, Durango, Salinas

Personal and Professional Events

- Reformatory officially reaccredited

Nov.   Sought therapy in Grand Rapids after a serious staff assault

Nov.   Family Thanksgiving in Ionia

Dec.   Picked up Salem to stay with us while Kristy studied for her pharmacy degree at Ferris

Dec.   Kristy introduced "bake-ahead" style of cookie day; while some baking still happened, many cookies were brought ready to be frosted or already finished; I continued to provide fudges; instead of ending late evening, we wrapped up by 5:00 p.m. or so.

1997

Michigan Department of Corrections (MDOC) Positions

Jul. 1986–Jul. 2001:

- Warden, Michigan Reformatory, Ionia

Boards

1987-2001:   Lansing Community College Advisory

1988-2001:   Montcalm Community College Advisory

1992-2001:   Michigan Women's Studies Association Friends

1993-2001:   Independent Bank

Conferences

Jan.   ACA Indianapolis

Aug.   ACA Orlando. Kay Wells and I stayed at Edna's Lake Wales home.

Speeches/Presentations/Articles

Feb.   State Employee Retirees Association, Ionia, "Reformatory Overview"

Feb.   Heartlands, "Non-Traditional Work"

Mar.   Ionia Intermediate School, "District Impact of a Prison in a Community"

Mar.   University of Michigan

Apr.   Calvin College, "Reformatory Overview"

Apr.   Kent, "Juvenile"

May   Greenville High School

May   Newaygo Alternative Ed.

Oct.   MSU Corrections student organization, "Corrections as a Career"

Oct.   Grand Rapids Women's Resource Center, "Corrections as a Career"

Nov.   Lansing Community College, "Corrections as a Career"

Nov.   Transport of prisoners for public presentations ends due to the need for a custody officer present.

Travels

Mar.   Travel to San Francisco, LA, San Diego, Houston. Saw sandhill cranes along the Platte in NE; visited with Orlu in CO; Frank and Mary Buchko in Sparks, NV; Karen Gibson and Bill's old Marine buddy, Ed

Kroll, in San Francisco; saw *Phantom of the Opera* there and enjoyed it immensely; saw Hale-Bopp (comet) while out strolling; drove south and stayed at Morro Bay, where we saw elephant seals and otters; visited with Russ and Jo, and then on to San Diego to meet Lychelle; Katie joined us there; on to Mexico for a time at Rosarita Beach; back to San Diego; then on the road again to Chet and Tekla's in Durango; weather was iffy, but we decided to try Wolf Creek Pass; turned back from there; went to Taos and took Raton Pass on I-25. Then snow hit and we spent the night in the Trinidad Methodist Church. Bill talked us into the lady chapel by telling the pastor that no one would get any sleep due to my snoring if we were in the sanctuary. At about 3:00 a.m., Bill was shaking the pew in what seemed a homicidal rage because my snoring, quite resonant in that space, was keeping him awake; I stayed awake for self-preservation from then on. I pulled kitchen duty in the a.m. and all the oranges we had brought from Russ and Jo's went into juice for the approximately sixty other stranded travelers.

Personal and Professional Events

Jan.   Lychelle born

Jan.   Three-day STP training conducted by RMI staff

Jun.   Tina visited Michigan.

Jun.   Three-day STP training conducted by RMI staff

Aug.   Russ and Jo visited Ionia.

1998

Michigan Department of Corrections (MDOC) Positions

Jul. 1986–Jul. 2001:

- Warden, Michigan Reformatory, Ionia

Boards

1987-2001:   Lansing Community College Advisory

1988-2001:   Montcalm Community College Advisory

1992-2001:   Michigan Women's Studies Association Friends

1993-2001:   Independent Bank

1998-2001:   Ferris State University Criminal Justice Advisory

Consulting

Dec.   "Quality Prison Management through Warden Interaction," Huntsville, Texas; squeezed in a visit w/Katie

Conferences

Jan. ACA San Antonio. Kay Wells went along.

May NAAWS, Lake of the Ozarks, MO

Aug. ACA Detroit

Speeches/Presentations/Articles

- WWICJJ Omaha, panelist, "Working Through Gender Wars to Create Partnerships"

Mar. University of Michigan, Buzz Alexander's class

Mar. MSU, Perry Johnson's class

Mar. MSU Business School, "Overview of Corrections"

Mar. Calvin College, "Juvenile Waiver"

Apr. STP training at the Oaks Correctional Facility in Manistee

Apr. Career Day at Portland St. Patrick's School

Apr. Cornerstone College, "Juvenile Waiver's Impact on Prisons"

May Field Office Administration Supervisors in Grand Rapids with Luella. Topics included mentoring.

Sept. Aquinas College, Robert Berles's class

Nov. MSU, Chris Smith's class, "How the Consent Decree Impacts Prison Operations"

Out-of-State Training Attended

Jun. NAC training for cognitive, problem-solving, and skills programs; "Thinking for a Change" presenter

Travels

Apr. Traverse City via Cadillac; lunch at Hermann's

Jun. Weekend with Gwen Andrew and Ruth Koehler in the Leelenau Peninsula

Jun. Old Goats (a group of older corrections retirees and their spouses) at Dick Nelson's in Grayling; drove separately so Bill could have extra time with his buddies

Jul. Bill drove to California while I stayed home.

Jul. Arnold Burke's 50th birthday party

Personal and Professional Events

Jan. Three-day STP training conducted by RMI staff

Feb. Salem stayed with us so Kristy could see the Chenille Sisters; when picked up, he said, "We should go to our house now!"

Feb.	Attended the Grand Rapids Symphony with Kay Wells, a birthday gift
Apr.	Family Easter in Ionia
Jul.	Salem at our place overnight so Kristy could study
Aug.	Tina, Brad, and Johannah visited
Aug.	John Bergman conducted role-playing training at the Reformatory.
Oct.	John and Kris marry.
Nov.	Much silliness around my 50th birthday; Luella engineered a party at a community liaison meeting at the Reformatory that included the city manager "returning" my lost pager, which had been flushed during a too-quick bathroom visit during consent decree experts' tour. That required a lost tool report, which made the fact public.
Nov.	Salem visited for the weekend while Kristy studied.

1999

Michigan Department of Corrections (MDOC) Positions

Jul. 1986–Jul. 2001:

- Warden, Michigan Reformatory, Ionia

Boards

1987-2001:	Lansing Community College Advisory
1988-2001:	Montcalm Community College Advisory
1992-2001:	Michigan Women's Studies Association Friends
1993-2001:	Independent Bank
1998-2001:	Ferris State University Criminal Justice Advisory

Consulting

Sept. "Sentencing and Managing Violent Offenders," Los Angeles, NIC-sponsored

Conferences

Jan.	ACA Nashville
May	NAAWS, Lake of the Ozarks, MO
Aug.	ACA Denver

Speeches/Presentations/Articles

Feb.	MSU Career Fair
Mar.	University of Michigan, "Working with Offenders"
Apr.	West Michigan city managers' meeting

Sept. National Conference on Sentencing and Managing Violent Offenders, Los Angeles, "Institution-Based Programming for Long-Term Offenders"

Travels

Jun. Weekend at Gwen Andrew and Ruth Koehler's up-north condo

Jul. San Diego to meet Mandalyn

Personal and Professional Events

Mar. The Reformatory reaccredited

Mar. Mandalyn born

2000

Michigan Department of Corrections (MDOC) Positions

Jul. 1986–Jul. 2001:

- Warden, Michigan Reformatory, Ionia

Boards

1987-2001: Lansing Community College Advisory

1988-2001: Montcalm Community College Advisory

1992-2001: Michigan Women's Studies Association Friends

1993-2001: Independent Bank

1998-2001: Ferris State University Criminal Justice Advisory

Honors

- Grand Valley State University Honorary Doctor of Laws

Conferences

- ACA San Antonio, Menger Hotel

Nov. WWICJJ, Houston

Speeches/Presentations/Articles

- NJ Correctional Association, "Women's Role in Correctional Facility Operations" with Luella Burke

Sept. Ionia Ladies' Literary Club, "Corrections Overview"

Travels

Jun. Weekend at Gwen and Ruth's up north

Oct. Houston

Personal and Professional Events

- Bill diagnosed with bladder cancer

Jan. Emceed Marjorie VanOchten's retirement party

Jun. Three-day STP training conducted by RMI staff

Jul. Three-day "Thinking for a Change" training conducted by RMI staff

Jul. Katie visited Ionia

Dec. Family Christmas at Chere and Mike's

2001

Michigan Department of Corrections (MDOC) Positions

Jul. 1986–Jul. 2001:

- Warden, Michigan Reformatory, Ionia

Boards

1987-2001: Lansing Community College Advisory

1988-2001: Montcalm Community College Advisory

1992-2001: Michigan Women's Studies Association Friends

1993-2001: Independent Bank

1998-2001: Ferris State University Criminal Justice Advisory

Honors

- Ferris State University Honorary Doctor of Public Service
- Michigan State University Criminal Justice Wall of Honor
- North American Association of Wardens and Superintendents' Warden of the Year

Conferences

Aug. ACA, NAAWS Warden of the Year, Philadelphia

Nov. AWEC w/ Sharon in New Orleans. My attempt to get her into a retirement mindset. Took the slow route on the Natchez Trace part of the way; visited Elvis's hometown; and then enjoyed New Orleans.

Travels

Jun. Glen Arbor with Gwen and Ruth

Aug. Columbus, OH, for genealogy research

Aug. Retirement trip through Canada to Vancouver and Victoria; on to Tina and Brad's via the Icefields Parkway; then Russ and Jo's (there for Sept. 11) and then on to San Diego and Houston. Home Sept 30.

Personal and Professional Events

Feb. John Bergman delivered role-playing training during three-day "Thinking for a Change" training

Feb. Aunt Vivian Gamble and cousin Marilyn visited

Apr. Family Easter at Edna's

Apr. Sleep study, breathing machine prescribed. Much relief for Bill and roommates at conferences.

Jun. Three-day "Thinking for a Change" training conducted by RMI staff

Jun. Pam retired.

Jun. Emergency response team members showed up at Ionia home to complain about the new warden; they were told they got me with three-and-a-half years' experience; they could return after their new boss had that much experience if they still had concerns; of course, I did not have another visit.

Oct. John and Kris's baby shower

Oct. With time to sew, I made Katie a velvet cloak and muff for cool weather parties.

2002

Boards

2002-2006: Ionia County Memorial Hospital

Consulting

- NIC planning session for Cultural Change in the Corrections Environment video

Conferences

Mar. MCA at Cabela's

May NAAWS Niagara Falls. Presented two sessions, one on women's role in the male-dominated correctional system, and the other on the impact of federal legislation on prison operations.

Nov. WWICJJ, Peabody Hotel, Memphis

Speeches/Presentations/Articles

Mar. CHANGE Keynote

Oct. Airstream travelers in Ionia topics: "First Woman Warden + Cognitive Work with Offenders"

Nov. Lakewood High School

Nov.   Ferris State University corrections class for Steve Poland

Travels

Apr.   Weekend up north

May   Chicago

Jun.   Glen Lake with Gwen and Ruth

Aug.   Rented two cabins at L'Daru Resort for Chris and Susie's visit—near Traverse City

Aug.   Pam to Indiana

Sept.   Bill to Houston

Nov.   Mt. Pleasant overnight

Personal and Professional Events

Jan.   Mason born

Mar.   Kristy's for family Easter

Jul.   Tina and Brad visited, as did Aunt Barb and Uncle Bob Ronksley.

Aug.   Chris and family visited.

Dec.   Christmas at Kristy's

2003

Boards

2002-2006:   Ionia County Memorial Hospital

Consulting

- Contributor to a NIC video, Cultural Change in the Corrections Environment
- NIC presenter for "Women's Leadership" for MDOC

Jan.   Developed a four-day seminar for National Academy of Corrections: "Positive Prison Culture"; about a dozen seasoned corrections professionals involved.

Honors

- Michigan Women's Hall of Fame

Conferences

Apr.   Criminal Justice Women of Michigan, Amway Hotel, Grand Rapids

May   BPW state conference, Boyne Mountain

Jun.   Michigan Hospital Association (MHA), Grand Hotel, Mackinac Island

Travels

Feb. California

May England, Scotland, Wales—gone two weeks

Aug. Rented two cabins at L'Daru Resort near Traverse City; John's family joined us for part of the week, then Kay Wells came for the rest.

Dec. Mt. Pleasant overnight

Personal and Professional Events

Mar. Tekla in Michigan, promoting one of her many books

Aug. Tina, Brad, and Johannah visited.

Sept. Bill diagnosed with chronic myeloid leukemia; he also had suffered prostate cancer

Oct. Luella and Sharon stayed with us for the Hall of Fame event.

2004

Boards

2002-2006: Ionia County Memorial Hospital

2004-2010: Ionia Community Library

Consulting

Oct. Assisted in developing the program and then presented for MDOC "Women's Leadership" training

Conferences

Mar. BPW Spring Board, Grayling

Jun. MHA, Grand Hotel, Mackinac Island. Bill attended; we then went on to Sault Ste. Marie for Sarah Caruso's wedding.

Aug. ACA Chicago

Sept. BPW Fall Board, Thomas Edison Inn, Port Huron

Oct. Association of Women Executives in Corrections (AWEC) and WWICJJ, Baltimore

Travels

Jan. Pam to LA for Russ's memorial service; Chris, Susie, and Katie there; Bill unable to travel

Apr. Mt. Pleasant overnight

Apr. Luella's overnight (Pam only)

Apr.	West Virginia to explore retirement possibilities; visited Sharon and her husband, Bill, as a bonus
May	Visited Kay Wells in Spring Lake, then on to Luella's in Scottville for an overnight (Pam only)
Jun.	Corvallis to visit Tina and Brad for Johannah's graduation
Jul.	Stayed at their cottage with Bill and Barb Eardley; went to the Old Goats' in Grayling
Aug.	Vacationed in Traverse City with Chris and Susie's family and John and Kris's family

Personal and Professional Events

Jan.	Bill's brother, Russ, passed.
Mar.	Stayed with Kristy after her surgery
Mar.	Red Hat events began; Lucy Hughes, a fellow library board member, introduced me to that group.
Jun.	Trevor born

2005

Boards

| 2002-2006: | Ionia County Memorial Hospital |
| 2004-2010: | Ionia Community Library |

Consulting

Jan.	MDOC "Thinking for a Change" facilitator training for community corrections with Deb Davis, Abe French, and Sandy Hoppough
Apr.	Planning in Washington, DC, for Moss Group activities in May 2005
May	Boise, ID, for the Moss Group: filming for the Prison Rape Elimination Act (PREA) and an eastern WA prison to problem-solve about a culture rife with sexual harassment
Nov.	MDOC "Women's Leadership" training in Tustin (no Luella)

Conferences

Jan.	ACA Nashville. Tina Moore raised the issue of creating an organization for WWICJJ—no success.
Mar.	BPW Spring Board, West Branch
Jun.	MHA Mackinac Island. I stayed at the Lakeview Hotel; visited newly widowed Barb Nelson in Grayling on the way home.
Aug.	ACA in Charlotte, North Carolina. Visited Barb and Bob Ronksley in Freedom, PA, on the way home.

| Sept. | NAAWS Cincinnati |
| Nov. | AWEC Ann Arbor |

Speeches/Presentations/Articles

Jan.	Ingham County parole training on cognitive programs
Oct.	NAAWS-sponsored training for middle managers with aspirations (in Cincinnati)
Nov.	Ferris State University corrections class

Travels

Mar.	Death Valley with Chris's family; very wet with the desert in bloom and kayakers able to navigate the desert floor; on to San Diego; home through Spring, Texas, to see Katie; a visit to Hot Springs, Arkansas, on the way home
Apr.	Chicago by train with John and family
May	Spain with Bill; joined by Luella, Lurline Baker Kent, and Marilyn Chandler Ford for Pego villa part
Jun.	Mt. Pleasant overnight
Jun.	Ludington for Luella and Arnold's 40th-anniversary party
Aug.	Tigers game with John and Kris, followed by a night at the Athenium with Bill
Aug.	Rented two cabins at Pineview Resort near Traverse City, and John's family joined us for part of the week, then Kay Wells came for the rest
Oct.	Mt. Pleasant overnight
Dec.	Mt. Pleasant overnight for an Independent Bank Christmas Party
Dec.	Late Christmas in San Diego (flew out); dinner at Emily Kime's (Bill's first wife); Magic Castle with David Stryker

Personal and Professional Events

Aug.	Tina visited for Mike and Sabrina McCloskey's wedding.
Nov.	Stayed with Mason and Trevor while John and Kris got away to Miami and the Bahamas for four days.
Dec.	Brad, Tina, and Johannah visited,

2006

Boards

| 2002-2006: | Ionia County Memorial Hospital |
| 2004-2010: | Ionia Community Library |

Consulting

- "Thinking for a Change" at Pugsley, w/Abe French

Mar. Planning for PREA filming for MDOC

Apr. "Thinking for a Change," MDOC

Jun. MDOC "Women's Leadership" training in Tustin (w/Luella)

Jul. "Thinking for a Change," MDOC

Sept. "Thinking for a Change," MDOC

Oct. MDOC "Women's Leadership" training in Tustin (w/Luella)

Oct. PREA filming for MDOC

Honors

- MDOC Corrections Officer class named Pamela K. Withrow Class

Conferences

Jan. ACA Nashville

Mar. BPW Spring Board

May BPW Conference

Aug. ACA North Carolina

Sept. AWEC/WWICJJ Phoenix. Katie joined Bill and me, and she and Bill got in a side trip to Las Vegas.

Oct. BPW Fall Board

Oct. Michigan Women's Hall of Fame dinner, Novi, Mary Esther Daddazio induction

Speeches/Presentations/Articles

- MDOC Pugsley Correctional Facility, "Thinking for a Change," with Abe French
- MDOC training for prisoner release initiative
- Minority Advisory Panel, "Women of Color"
- MDOC training for wardens, with Kurt Jones

Sept. WWICJJ presented "To Be or Not to Be...One of the Boys" with Luella

Apr. Schoolcraft College fundraiser, spoke on first woman warden experience

Oct. MSU sociology class presentation, Luella's and my variation of "To Be..."

Travels

Mar.	Nashville for AWEC Strategic Planning

Mar. Nashville for AWEC Strategic Planning

Apr. Travel to Chicago by train with John, Kris, Mason, and Trevor

May Visited Kay Wells, then traveled to Bellaire Inn for a long weekend, including Old Goats gathering

Jul. Saugatuck overnight for theatre performance there

Jul. Meijer Gardens for Nickel Creek

Aug. Mt. Pleasant for the Native American Museum, and Big Rapids for the Jim Crow Museum with Lucy Hughes

Aug. Headed for Chet and Tekla's on the way to CA; Concorde blew up near Ft. Morgan, CO, so we bought a Chrysler 300M. Bill's favorite car ever. Quick visit with Jo and on to San Diego; the return home included AWEC and WWICJJ conferences in Phoenix. Katie joined us there and she and I each flew to our homes and Bill drove home solo. He got stopped in a southern state just west of the Mississippi and questioned about his travels. He later figured out he was driving a car that might be thought to be a drug dealer's which had a Michigan license plate and a decal from Colorado. He loved to tell that story.

Oct. Grand Rapids for dinner with Luella and Arnold at San Chez

Nov. Coldwater for doggie graduation at Carol Howes's prison

2007

Other Ongoing Employment

- Instructor, with John Cordell, Ferris State University

Boards

2004-2010: Ionia Community Library

Consulting

Feb. "Thinking for a Change," MDOC, Coldwater

Conferences

Jan. ACA Tampa

Apr. NAAWS Pittsburgh

Aug. ACA Kansas City with Luella; visited Springfield, IL, and the Lincoln Museum. There also was a Frank Lloyd Wright home.

Oct. BPW, Sault Ste. Marie, Kewadin Casino

Travels

Feb.	Luella and Pam to Saginaw
May	Old Goats Traverse City
Jul.	Dearborn for NOW conference to sell MWSA store items; stayed in Ann Arbor at Burnt Toast B&B

Personal and Professional Events

May	Matt and Rebecca McCloskey marry.
Jul.	Chris's family flew into Chicago, and Bill and I took the train there and enjoyed visiting the Windy City for three days, then all took the train back to K-zoo for a visit with Susie's friend from college; they spent a week in Ionia with visits to Edna, Kris, and Salem, and John's family as well as a visit with Kay Wells for a day at the beach. John and family joined in for that, as well as a canoe trip on the K-zoo River.
Aug.	Bunion surgery and no weight-bearing for eight weeks, which got extended and then converted to a walking cast. No driving. Kneeling scooter about did me in! Lu took me to Tina Moore's wedding, hauling the scooter in and out of the car.
Nov.	Celebrated Edna's 80th birthday at her home with family and friends; John donated a harp session he had won, so we had elegant harp music. Matt announced they were having a baby, so extra cause for celebration. Chris Kime and Marilyn and Kerm attended.

2008

Boards

2004-2010:   Ionia Community Library

Conferences

May	BPW Spring Board, Amway Hotel, Grand Rapids
Aug.	ACA New Orleans w/Luella. Sharon and John were there, too, traveling separately. Overnight in Nashville going down. Came back via Arkansas to visit Luella's kin there (Dry Prong), and Indiana (past the farm and then visited Marilyn Gamble after her stroke).
Oct.	AWEC/WWICJJ in Des Moines w/Luella. Amana Colonies as a side trip; Luella received the Susan Hunter Award; Luella and I presented "To Be or Not To Be...One of the Boys" to a packed room.

Travels

| Mar. | Olivet College with Tekla and Luella, then on to Coldwater to see Carol Howes's dog program |
| Jul. | Great Wolf and Boyne with John and family; Marsha Foresman and I |

squeezed in a visit at that time. (I think this was when she confided that Ray had early-onset Alzheimer's—a confidence I maintained and which strained my relationship with Luella when she found out years later that I had known and not told her.)

Aug.   Grand Rapids for an overnight at the Amway to celebrate our 22nd anniversary

Aug.   Travel to Indiana with Tina, Chere, Mike, and Kristy for cousins' visit and to meet with Ron Gamble about Withrow Acres

Aug.   Travel to Luella's to plan for WWICJJ presentation; pajama party there for Denise, Adria, and me and an afternoon visit with Marsha. Watched an Obama debate with Luella's friends and enjoyed an afternoon chat on the deck with Denise while Luella went to a meeting.

Nov.   Bittersweet 60th-birthday celebration at the Book Cadillac in Detroit. Edna and I had planned to go there, but her death nixed that. Bill and I did go, and stayed on the 20th floor with views of downtown, the Ambassador Bridge, and Canada. Saw my first live opera (*Madame Butterfly*) and had dinner at Fishbones. Visited the DIA before heading home. The significance of the Book was that Edna had confided that she believed I was conceived there when she and Charles enjoyed a jazz weekend in Detroit before it was time to start spring farming.

Nov.   Indiana visit to transfer the farmland to Withrow Acres

Personal and Professional Events

Mar.   Tekla spoke at Olivet College; Lu, Denise, Adria, and I listened to the speech, then had dinner with Pat Caruso, Sue Kohloff, and Jeri Ann Sherry at Denise's; after they left, we had a Network sleepover and looked at photos I'd brought and talked and laughed and were asleep by eleven. On the 20th, Luella, Tekla, and I went to Coldwater to see Carol's dog program, and there I got a call that Edna was at Sparrow Hospital and that I should come there as soon as I could.

Mar.   Edna passed.

Apr.   Bill hospitalized (Apr.4-Apr.9) after oxycontin and fentanyl interaction caused hallucinations. Finally got him back to normal and ready for back surgery on May 20.

May   Bill's first back surgery

Aug.   Gall bladder surgery

Sept.   Katie visited.

Sept.   Final distribution of property and possessions from the trust and Edna's home

Fall   Volunteered for the Obama campaign. Ionia had an actual office and I did data entry, made phone calls, knocked on doors, and delivered yard signs. Felt righteous when he won.

Oct.   John and Kris to Las Vegas for their 10th wedding anniversary, and I had the boys for six days.

Oct.   Kristy's foot surgery, and I helped her before heading to Des Moines

---

2009

Boards

2004-2010:   Ionia Community Library

Conferences

May   BPW conference at Boyne Mountain. Kris brought Mason and Trevor to enjoy the water park while John was off in Washington, DC, at an Honor Guard function; Mary Esther Daddazio in attendance.

Aug.   ACA Nashville

Oct.   BPW Fall Board

Travels

Jan.   Traveled by train from Battle Creek to Albany, OR, to visit Tina and family; spent the night in Battle Creek with Bill when I returned.

Feb.   Big Rapids for lunch with Luella

Mar.   Drove to San Diego, flew Katie out there, then on to San Francisco and stayed at the Beresford Hotel and drove home.

May   Chicago by train with John, Kris, Mason, and Trevor. (Bill stayed home with intestinal issues.)

May   Took Bob Berles with us to the Old Goats at the Elks Club in Traverse City

Jul.   Travel to Pennsylvania for Diana's (oldest Ronksley cousin) memorial; started in Detroit with a stay at the Athenium Hotel, a birthday gift for Bill, then on to the Toledo Art Museum, and to Cleveland for a Tigers' game, then to Freedom to stay with Barb and Bob. In addition to the memorial for Diana, we had a baptism for Tom and Donna Ronksley's granddaughter and a birthday party for Kay and Bill Heidkamp's son, Kris. What an emotional rollercoaster!

Sept.   Luella's overnight

Oct.   Cadillac for a visit with Luella and Marsha Foresman

Oct.   Stratford, Canada, for plays

Oct.   Tina visited for two cousins' reunions. First in Indiana and second in Ohio with Pennsylvania cousins and their parents. Ironically, cousin Dennis Macy passed late in the month after enjoying the reunion.

Personal and Professional Events

May   John Paul (JP) and Karen McCloskey marry

2010

Boards

2004-2010:   Ionia Community Library

Conferences

Mar.   BPW Spring Board

Apr.   NAAWS conference in Niagara Falls with Luella

May   BPW conference

Speeches/Presentations/Articles

Apr.   MSU class

Nov.   Davenport class

Travels

Apr.   Shipshewana, Indiana, bus tour

Apr.   After a NAAWS conference, Luella and I traveled to see Mary Bogan in New York and on to Maine to see Patty Barnhart at her prison there.

May   Last Old Goats

May   Turkeyville for lunch and theatre with Red Hats

Jun.   Indiana farm visit with Tina

Jul.   Boyne with the San Diego family joined by the Cordell family

Aug.   Mt. Pleasant overnight

Aug.   Turkeyville for lunch and theatre with Red Hats

Oct.   Macy cousins' reunion in Indiana

Oct.   Visit with Elaine Yakura (MSU) and Marsha Foresman in Cadillac

Oct.   Red Hats to Art Prize and Meijer Gardens in Grand Rapids

---

2011

Conferences

May   NAAWS Baton Rouge. Attended the Angola Rodeo with Luella; stayed in Nashville on the way there; came back via Arkansas to visit Luella's kin (Dry Prong); I then took the train home from Memphis.

Sept.   AWEC in Raleigh; Luella and I drove with a side trip to Mt. Airy

(Mayberry, RFD). Met Sharon, who received the Susan Hunter Award (I got to introduce her), then we went on to Ocracoke Island.

Speeches/Presentations/Articles

Nov.   Davenport class

Travels

May   Disney World with Cordell family

Jul.   Ludington for Luella's 70th

Aug.   Toured Dow Gardens and had dinner in Mt. Pleasant followed by an overnight

Sept.   Pittsburgh to visit Barb and Bob Ronksley; met Luella there and traveled on to Raleigh, NC, for AWEC; then Ocracoke with Sharon

Oct.   Turkeyville for lunch and theatre with Red Hats

Personal and Professional Events

Jan.   Right knee replaced

2012

Boards

2012-2018:   Michigan Women's Studies Association

Conferences

Sept.   AWEC

Travels

Feb.   Caberfae w/John, Mason, and Trevor; they skied and I knitted.

Apr.   Luella's overnight

Apr.   Indiana farm visit with Mason and Trevor

Apr.   Jim Crow Museum with the Red Hats

May   Red Hats Museum Day

Jun.   I traveled to San Diego w/John's family for Keeler's graduation; we rented a van and then drove up the coast to Tina and Brad's, then Portland, including a visit to Powell's bookstore, and then the plane home for the Cordells. Tina and I drove the van back to San Diego and both flew home from there.

Aug.   Turkeyville for lunch and theatre with Red Hats

Aug.   Overnight in Ann Arbor with Bill to celebrate our 26th anniversary

Sept.   Red Hats riverboat adventure

Oct.   Red Hats to Coopersville

Nov.   Chelsea overnight with Bill for Purple Rose play

Personal and Professional Events

Jun.   Bill's colostomy

2013

Boards

2012-2018:   Michigan Women's Studies Association

Travels

Jul.   Mackinac Island and Sault Ste. Marie with the Kime crew plus Kristy. She had loaned us her camper for the girls to stay in; given Lychelle's cat allergy, she couldn't stay in the house. Bill could not travel because of his back, so Kris was my roomie.

Aug.   Indiana with Tina and Brad; stayed at the Union at Purdue, and Kay and Bill and Tom and Donna joined us. Had a farm visit as well as reunion with Macy cousins.

Oct.   Savannah by bus with fifty other old folks, mostly from Ionia. Doris Lovato was my roomie, and Norma Kilpatrick and Linda Hood were others I knew prior to the trip.

Personal and Professional Events

Jul.   Finished remodeling project on Ionia home—bamboo floors in living room, dining room, and kitchen, and new shower in master bath, with tile floor in that area

Aug.   Tina and Brad visited; after an Indiana trip, we gathered at Chere and Mike's to meet Max's baby sister, Lizzie, and visit with the rest of the McCloskeys, minus Matt's family.

Sept.   Bill's second back surgery

Nov.   Spent my 65th birthday at the Amerihost Inn in Ionia after bad storms resulted in lost power

---

2014

Boards

2012-2018:   Michigan Women's Studies Association

Conferences

May   BPW Chelsea

Travels

Aug.   Luella's overnight for PEO talk

Aug.   Indiana farm visit

Sept.   Freedom, PA, for Bob Ronksley's funeral

Oct.   Indiana farm visit

Oct.   Red Hats Frankenmuth visit

Oct.   Day trip to Battle Creek casino

Dec.   Met Luella in Muskegon to celebrate my birthday and Christmas

Personal and Professional Events

Jul.   Move to E. Lansing condo

Aug.   Katie visit—ten days

2015

Boards

2012-2018:   Michigan Women's Studies Association

Travels

Feb.   Day trip to Battle Creek casino

Mar.   Meijer Gardens for the butterflies

May   Turkeyville for lunch and theatre with Red Hats

Jun.   Indiana farm visit

Jun.   Ludington for Luella and Arnold's 50th-anniversary celebration

Jul.   Traveled by train to Tina and Brad's for Johannah and Will's wedding; arrived early to prep for the at-home event

Aug.   Red Hats Frankenmuth

Sept.   Meijer Gardens with the Cordell family

Sept.   Met Luella in Grand Rapids for Art Prize and Meijer Gardens tours

Oct.   Karen McCloskey arranged tickets for *Wait, Wait...Don't Tell Me!* in Ann Arbor; Kristy and I enjoyed a great dinner with her there, too.

Personal and Professional Events

Apr.   Stayed with Mason and Trevor while John and Kris cruised

May   Chris, Keeler, Lychelle, and Mandalyn visited for one week (Susie had no vacation time). My concern about sleeping arrangements was resolved with the girls in the guest room, Keeler on the downstairs couch, and Chris on the torture bed in the laundry/workshop area downstairs.

May Left knee replaced

May Miller Homes remodeled guest bath and added half-bath downstairs

May Ollie (cat) was euthanized at MSU after abdominal cancer was found

Jun. Replaced carpet and tiled kitchen and dining area

2016

Boards

2012-2018: Michigan Women's Studies Association

Travels

Jan. Unplanned trip to San Diego for a Kime family emergency

Apr. Indiana farm visit

May Mother's Day at the Grand Hotel on Mackinac Island with the Cordell family. Bill was unable to travel, so we took advantage of a special w/ five to the room, which included a balcony. We were not there much, enjoying a carriage and fort tour, bicycling, etc. The boys thought the food was great and managed the loooong dinner evening quite agreeably.

May Portland and Albany by train with Sharon. Powell's bookstore for three days while staying at the McMenamins Crystal Hotel, and then on to Tina and Brad's. Home via Coast Starlight and California Zephyr.

May Indiana for cousin Mark Naylor's memorial (gone at fifty-six with lung cancer); Chere and Mike came, too.

May Pittsburgh for Barb Ronksley's memorial service; Kristy came with me for this one.

Jul. Toured Bellamy Creek Correctional Facility in Ionia

Sept. Traveled to Tekla's and stayed there with Denise, Luella, and Adria. I went by train to Albuquerque; others flew. Rented a car and drove to Tekla's. Ended the trip in Taos with just Luella and Denise.

Personal and Professional Events

May Bill surgery—detatched retina

Dec. Bill to ICU with dehydration; Dec. 18 overnight in GP bed; Dec. 19 home; Bill told me he had had a good run and would not agree to dialysis if it came to that.

Dec. Parathyroid removal

Dec. Bill having difficulty breathing; to ER by ambulance; I drove to Sparrow against doc's orders; John drove me home and Chere and Mike took me in the next day. Christmas dinner at the condo w/ John and family on the 23rd. Christmas day at Sparrow. Home Dec. 28; diagnosis: congestive heart failure

---

2017

Boards

2012-2018: Michigan Women's Studies Association

Speeches/Presentations/Articles

Mar. MDOC podcast for Women's History Month

Travels

Apr. Indiana farm visit

May Mooville with the Red Hats

Jul. Traveled by train (Southwest Chief) to Mandalyn's graduation with Mason and Trevor. The original plan did not include them, so the first night they were in coach; not good. We switched and they got my roomette the second night; much better. Coming home, we had a family bedroom (in-room bathroom) and they thought that was even better. Great visit with the Kimes.

Aug. Red Hats lighthouse tour

Sept. Saugatuck with Gladys Beckwith

Personal and Professional Events

Jul. We both got hearing aids. Wonderful changes to the world!

2018

Boards

2012-2018: Michigan Women's Studies Association

Travels

Apr. Meijer Gardens with the Cordell family to see the butterflies

May Traveled w/Gladys Beckwith by train (Empire Builder) to Portland. She and her daughter Chris explored Oregon beaches and I went on to Tina's. We met up there and returned home down the coast (Coast Starlight) and across the country on the California Zephyr.

Jul.	Cape Cod with Kristy, driving straight through both coming and going. Stayed at Tina and Brad's W. Falmouth home. Joined by John and his family; Yip, Karen, and Sean McCloskey; Will and Johannah; and Kristy's friend, Kris Taylor. Christopher stayed with Bill.
Jul.	Ludington with Denise for Arnold's 80th
Aug.	Indiana farm visit
Aug.	Luella and I went to Minneapolis via the Badger from Ludington for Pat Caruso's ER Cass Award at ACA. Drove home through the Upper Peninsula and visited Bob and Lynn Lecureux as they were preparing for the sale of their home on the St. Mary's River. Bittersweet visit. Along the way, we stayed at the Landmark in Marquette (good beds and Luella liked it) and the Ramada in Sault Ste. Marie, which had been the Ojibway in our Presidents' Day weekend ski-visit era. That property had gone downhill, but we had a good breakfast at Frank's Place. Beata stayed with Bill.
Sept.	Kristy and I visited Chere and Mike's cottage in NE Michigan and celebrated Kristy's birthday there.
Sept.	Mason, Trevor, and I visited Indiana for a surprise party for cousin, Carol Royer, and her honey, John.
Nov.	Luella and Arnold, Sharon and Bill, and Denise and I went to the Euro Bistro in Grand Rapids to celebrate my 70th birthday. Plumbing problems there sent us to Noto's, where we had a fine dinner; Bill was unable to join us.

Personal and Professional Events

Nov.	Bill fell at the bedside; he said his feet just slipped out from under him. He did not hit his head, and, between the two of us, we managed to get him back into bed.
Nov.	Another ambulance ride to Sparrow; this time with abdominal pain. I was also concerned about his mental state—he'd gotten "lost" in the bedroom in the night trying to find the bathroom; asked me how to brush his teeth and garbled and searched for words. Time was jumbled also.
Nov.	Bill woke me about 4:00 a.m. and said he was done. We talked for a while and then slept some. I awoke to him sitting up in bed making casting motions. Then he tried to get out of bed. I told him I did not want him to fall again, and he asked me to call John so he could go to the bathroom instead of using the urinal. John came and saw what a mess Bill was mentally and said he'd talked with Chris and perhaps it was time we started the hospice process; I called Dr. Gaumer's office and discovered she was also Sparrow's hospice doc; she said she'd try to get someone out that afternoon. Kristy arrived and she was there when the intake RN discussed the hospice process. John stayed with

Bill while I signed the paperwork; initial meds were delivered. The intake RN even changed Bill's colostomy pouch!

Nov. Hospice RN visited with more meds; hospital bed was delivered; tech got Bill cleaned up; John again there for support. Christopher and Tina both decided to come to help. Chere brought chicken stew and visited for a while.

Nov. Chris and Tina arrived; John and Chere again present; the Cordell crew came for dinner and the boys and I played cribbage. (Saddleback and Thai Princess provided dinner.) Chris called the RN to shut off Bill's pacemaker at Kris Cordell's suggestion. Bill was crying and trying to get out of bed during Chris's night shift. He woke me and we called the RN, who upped the dosage of Ativan. Also suggested giving 50 mg. Benadryl crushed in solution. Bill slept soundly from then on.

Dec. Tina, Chris, and I rotated care for Bill. John was there for support as was Chere (and Kristy as her work permitted). Tina and Chere shopped for and made a pot roast dinner.

Dec. I had the 4:00 a.m. to 8:00 a.m. shift and found Bill's body had cooled considerably; his head and extremities were very cool. He was still breathing and seemed peaceful. I sat in the rocker, held his hand, and played pan-pipe music and the choral chant he had liked so much. I talked about how wonderful our life had been together and told him he could go when he was ready. Kristy picked me up to go work out and, when we returned, we saw Chris out walking and knew Bill was gone. The RN on call was in Carson City, so didn't get to us right away, but accepted Chris's estimate that Bill had passed about 8:30 a.m. After she got Bill cleaned up and ready for the funeral home people, I called Lake in Ionia and they came and took his body for cremation. Chris and Tina stayed a bit longer and then returned to their lives and I began to learn about being a widow.

2019

Travels

May Traveled by train (California Zephyr) to wine country for Lychelle's graduation from Sonoma State.

Personal and Professional Events

Mar. Two weeks in Holt while John and Kris cruised for their 20th-anniversary celebration (a few months late). Bought a 2016 RAV4 hybrid while there and loaned the Flex to Mason while retaining title and paying for insurance. Took Trevor out to drive the new car as part of his driver training. We visited Chere and Mike and Kris and Salem and ended the drive at Culver's. He was a good and careful driver. When Mason tried driving it the next day, he complained that it did not have the horsepower of the Flex.

Jun. Bill's memorial was held at Kristy's, Quaker-style as he had requested. In addition to family, Luella and Arnold Burke and Sharon Johnson Rion and Bill Rion attended, as did Beata Zarebski and her daughters, Sara and Amanda, and Gary and Kay Wells's sons.

2020

Consulting

- State Appellate Defenders Office: writing reports about lifers whose crimes were committed before they turned eighteen

Travels

Mar. Costa Rica with Tina for an ecotour which started in San Jose, continued through the Cloud Forest in Monte Verde, then a dry forest area (rafting there), and on to the tropical forest farther west, ending on the Pacific coast. The hotel there was the base for a boat tour and a visit to a pottery cooperative. Flew home from Liberia.

Aug. Visited Luella and Arnold in Scottville

Personal and Professional Events

Mar. Stayed with Mason and Trevor while John and Kris vacationed

2021

Consulting

- State Appellate Defenders Office: writing reports about lifers whose crimes were committed before they turned eighteen

Speeches/Presentations/Articles

Mar. Michigan Unemployment Insurance Lunch and Learn panelist for Women's History Month

Dec. Testified for the first time in a case seeking a term of years for a prisoner sentenced to life for a crime he committed when he was younger than eighteen.

Travels

Jun. Ludington for Arnold's funeral

Jun.	Amtrak to Oregon to visit Tina and Brad, Johannah, Will, and Henry; on to San Diego to celebrate Keeler's and Mandalyn's college graduations; to San Francisco and a visit with Karen Gibson
Jul.	Nashville, to celebrate Luella's 80th birthday
Oct.	Nashville and Burns, TN, for Bill Rion's celebration of life; home through Indiana. Carol hosted a cousins' breakfast.

Personal and Professional Events

Mar.	Arnold Burke passed.
Jun.	Arnold's memorial service; Denise and I roomed together at the Greiner Motel—it had not aged well.
Jun.	Traveled to Albany and Eugene, OR; Los Angeles; San Diego; and San Francisco
Jun.	Katie passed.
Sept.	Luella visited Michigan.
Oct.	Traveled to Nashville to stay with Luella for Bill Rion's celebration of life; stayed with Sharon after relatives left, drove home through Indiana, where Carol Royer hosted a cousins' breakfast.

2022

Consulting

- State Appellate Defenders Office: writing reports about lifers whose crimes were committed before they turned eighteen

Travels

Jun.	Ludington for Arnold's funeral
Jul.	Hosted John and family for two weeks and Chris and family for one week in Steamboat Springs, CO. I traveled across Lake Michigan on the Badger after staying with Joan Nelson and enjoying a traditional liver dinner at the Bungalow in Manistee. Met up with the Cordell crew and toured Mt. Rushmore and Crazy Horse. Chris, Susie, and Mandalyn drove, with Lychelle and Keeler flying in to celebrate his birthday. Visited with Deb Davis; also with Carol Royer and other Indiana cousins on the way home.

Personal and Professional Events

| Jul. | Luella visited for a surprise for Tekla at a Brighton dinner she thought Denise and I were attending. Overnight in Brighton and lunch with Luella's friends. Drove back roads to and from East Lansing. Lunch later in the week with Denise and Susan Kohloff, and a dinner with Regina Armstrong. Then Luella went on to Ludington for a visit. |

Sept. Luella passed peacefully in Tennessee. I was glad to have had one last time to say goodbye when I went to Ludington to start my Steamboat Springs trip. We sat on the beach and watched Lake Michigan waves roll in and recalled the adventures we had shared and told each other how much we had loved our times together. Her life will be celebrated in Ludington in October.

ABOUT THE AUTHOR

Pam Withrow was born into an Indiana farm family near the midpoint of the 20th century, moved to Michigan in the turbulent '60s, and was a pioneering woman in the Michigan Department of Corrections. After a shotgun marriage, she returned to college, divorced, became a welfare mother, and completed a BA at Michigan State University. With the help of a bus driver boyfriend, she began work with the Michigan Department of Corrections in 1976. After only two years, she was promoted to become the first woman to supervise a camp for male felons. This was followed by work as the housing deputy inside Jackson prison, which led to her appointment as the first woman to head a male prison, the Michigan Dunes Correctional Facility. She then served as the warden of the Michigan Reformatory, one of three penitentiaries in the state, for the final fifteen years of her career. She introduced cognitive work with prisoners while at the Reformatory, and it is now used throughout the department.

She was named Warden of the Year by the North American Association of Wardens and Superintendents, received honorary doctorates from Grand Valley and Ferris State Universities, and was inducted into the Michigan Women's Hall of Fame.

She does not regret her early retirement from prison work, reminding anyone who will listen that spending time with family and friends beats going to work.

Made in the USA
Monee, IL
27 November 2022

18744189R00114